GLOBETROTTER

COSTA RICAN SPANISH
In Your Pocket

**NEW
HOLLAND**

GLOBETROTTER™

First edition published in 2005
by New Holland Publishers Ltd
London • Cape Town • Sydney •
Auckland
10 9 8 7 6 5 4 3 2

website:
www.newhollandpublishers.com

Garfield House, 86 Edgware Road
London W2 2EA
United Kingdom

80 McKenzie Street
Cape Town 8001
South Africa

14 Aquatic Drive
Frenchs Forest, NSW 2086
Australia

218 Lake Road
Northcote, Auckland
New Zealand

Publishing Manager (UK):
Simon Pooley
Publishing Manager (SA):
Thea Grobbelaar
Cover design: Nicole Bannister
Illustrator: Marisa Galloway
Editor: Thea Grobbelaar
Translator: José Hares
Consultant: Lynn Zinn
Proofreader: Manuel Lijó Pedro

Reproduction by Resolution, Cape Town
Printed and bound by Replika Press,
India

Cover photograph: *A keel-billed
toucan in Tortuguero National Park,
Costa Rica.*

CONTENTS

This PHRASE BOOK is thematically colour-coded for easy use and is organized according to the situation you're most likely to be in when you need it. The fairly comprehensive DICTIONARY section consists of two parts – English/Spanish and Spanish/English.

To make speaking Spanish easy, we encourage our readers to memorize some general PRONUNCIATION rules (*see* page 8). After you have familiarized yourself with the basic tools of the language and the rudiments of Spanish GRAMMAR (see page 14), all you need to do is turn to the appropriate section of the phrase book and find the words you need to make yourself understood. If the selection is not exactly what you're looking for, consult the dictionary for other options.

Just to get you started, here are some Spanish expressions you might have heard, read or used at some time: *adiós, por favor, gracias, hasta mañana, siesta.* Even if you are unfamiliar with these words and would rather not try to say them out loud, just remain confident, follow our easy advice and practise a little, and you will soon master useful phrases for everyday life. Speak slowly and enunciate carefully and your counterpart is likely to follow suit.

Some Spanish words, especially those ending in -ion, are pronounced differently from their English equivalents (e.g. extensión – *ex-ten-syon*), or else changed just slightly (mayonnaise – *mayonesa*), though their meanings remain clear. Nowadays many English terms are used in Spanish, especially in business, sport and leisure activities, so everyone will know what you mean when you say things like 'laptop', 'golf' and 'tennis'.

A section on HOLIDAYS AND FESTIVALS (*see* page 82) provides some background knowledge so that you know what you're celebrating and why. There's no better way to learn a language than joining in some enjoyment!

The brief section on manners, mannerisms and ETIQUETTE (*see* page 76) can help you make sense of the people around you. Make an effort to view your host country and its people tolerantly – that way you will be open to the new experience and able to enjoy it.

Learning a new language can be a wonderful but frightening experience. It is not the object of this book to teach you perfect Spanish, but rather to equip you with just enough knowledge for a successful holiday or business trip. Luckily you are unlikely to be criticized on your grammatical correctness when merely asking for directions. The most important thing is to make yourself understood. To this end a brief section on grammar and a guide to pronunciation have been included in this book. There is, however, no substitute for listening to native speakers.

Before you leave, it might be a good idea to familiarize yourself with the sections on Pronunciation, Grammar and Etiquette. This can easily be done en route to your destination. You will also benefit from memorizing a few important phrases before you go.

The sections of the Phrase Book are arranged by topic for quick reference. Simply go to the contents list (*see* page 3) to find the topic you need. The Dictionary section (*see* page 88) goes both ways, helping you to understand and be understood.

Abbreviations have been used in those instances where one English word could be interpreted as more than one part of speech, e.g. 'smoke' (a noun, the substance coming from a fire) and 'smoke' (a verb, what one would do with a cigarette). Here is a list of these and some other abbreviations used in this book:

vb	verb
n	noun
adj	adjective
adv	adverb
prep	preposition
pol	polite
fam	familiar (informal)
elec	electric/al
med	medical
anat	anatomy
rel	religion

The gender and number of Spanish nouns have been specified as follows:

m	masculine
f	feminine
pl	plural

Spanish is a phonetic language, so with a bit of practice you can soon read most of it. Many letters are pronounced much like the English equivalent. The English words given here contain sounds that approximate Spanish sounds.

VOWELS
VOCALES

- a – like the **a** in f**a**ther – *gato*
- e – like the **e** in l**e**t – *me*
- i – like the **ee** in m**ee**t – *hijo*
- o – like the **o** in **o**rder – *yo*
- u – like the **oo** in f**oo**t, but shorter – *tu*

NB The letter **u** following a **g** or a **q** is silent, unless marked with an umlaut – *desagüe*.

DIPHTHONGS
DIPTONGOS

- ai – like the **i** in b**i**te – *bailar*
- ay – like the **i** in b**i**te – *hay*
- au – like the **ow** in c**ow** – *audiencia*
- ei – like the **ey** in th**ey** – *reina*
- ey – like the **ey** in th**ey** – *ley*
- eu – sound each vowel separately – *Europa*
- ia – like the **ya** in **ya**rd – *enviar*

- **ie** – like the **ye** in **yes** – *tiene*
- **io** – like the **yo** in **yore** – *junio*
- **iu** – like **you** – *viuda*
- **oi** – like the **oy** in **toy** – *boicot*
- **oy** – like the **oy** in **toy** – *estoy*
- **ua** – like the **wa** in **want** – *cuando*
- **uay** – like the **wi** in **wise** – *Uruguay*
- **ue** – like the **wea** in **weather** – *bueno*
- **uey** – like the **wai** in **wait** – *buey*
- **ui** – like the **wee** in **week** – *suizo*
- **uo** – like the **wo** in **woke** – *cuota*

If a vowel is marked with an accent (e.g. é, á), it indicates that this syllable is stressed.

CONSONANTS
CONSONANTES

- **b** – see **v**
- **c** – like the **k** in **keep** – *cabeza*
- **c** – before **e** and **i**, like the **s** in **site** (used in this book) or like the **th** in **thin** – *cielo*
- **ch** – like the **ch** in **chop** – *mucho*
- **d** – between vowels or at the end of a word, it sounds like the **th** in **father** – *cada*
- **g** – before **e** and **i**, it sounds like the **ch** in **loch** (represented as **kh** in this book) – *gente*

- **g** – like the g in **g**et – *gato*
- **h** – the letter h is always silent – *hola*
- **j** – like the ch in lo**ch** (represented as **kh** in this book) – *jueves*
- **ll** – like the y in **y**et – *silla*
- **ñ** – like the **ny** in ca**ny**on – *niño*
- **q** – like the c in **c**ar – *querer*
- **r** – rolled as in Scots – *pero*
- **rr** – a lengthened rolled r sound – *perro*
- **s** – always pronounced like the s in **s**oap, never like the s in ea**s**y – *mesa*
- **v** – at the beginning of a word or after m or n, like the b in **b**ird (but less percussive) – *viento*
- **v** – in any other position, like a cross between the English **b** and **v** (with the lips barely meeting) – *mover*
- **z** – like the th in **th**ing – *azul*

There are variations in the pronunciation of Spanish, depending on where it is spoken, e.g. Latin America, Andalucía or the rest of Spain. The letter **z**, for example, could sound like the **th** in **th**ing, but in Latin America it would be pronounced like the **s** in **s**imple. Wherever you are, you will soon know how to pronounce the words simply by listening to the local people speaking.

Practise a few phrases in Spanish (the stressed syllables are underlined):

Buenos días
bwe-nos dee-yas
Good day

¡Hola!
o-la
Hello!

Adiós
ad-yos
Goodbye

¿Habla inglés?
ab-la in-gless
Do you speak English?

Hable despacio, por favor
ab-leh des-paa-syoh, por fa-vor
Please speak slowly

No entiendo
noh ent-yen-doh
I don't understand

¿Cómo está usted?
koh-moh es-ta oos-ted
How are you? (polite)

¿Qué tal?
keh tal
How are you? (familiar)

Bien, gracias
byen, graa-syass
Fine, thanks!

Quiero ...
kyeh-roh
I'd like ...

¿Cómo dice?
ko-mo dee-seh
Pardon?

Por favor
por fa-vor

¡Gracias!
graa-syass
Thank you!

¡Lo siento!
  (¡Disculpe!)
loh syen-toh
  (dis-cool-peh)
Sorry! Excuse me!

¿Por dónde están
  los servicios?
por don-deh es-tahn
  los ser-vee-syos
Where are the toilets?

¿Cuándo llega el
  tren?
kwan-doh yeh-gah
  el trenn
When does the train
  arrive?

¿Dónde está?
don-deh es-tah
Where is it?

¿Puedo ...?
pweh-doh
May I ...?

ayer
ah-yehr
yesterday

hoy
oy
today

mañana
ma-nya-na
tomorrow

¿Puedo llamar por
  teléfono?
pweh-doh yah-mahr
  por te-leh-foh-noh
May I use the phone?

The grammar section has deliberately been kept very brief as this is not a language course.

PERSONAL PRONOUNS
PRONOMBRES PERSONALES

Subject	
yo	I
tú	you (fam)
usted (ud.)	you (pol)
él, ella	he/she
nosotros/as	we
vosotros/as	you (pl fam)
ustedes (uds.)	you (pl pol)
ellos/ellas	they

Direct Object		Indirect Object	
me	me	(to) me	me
you	te (fam)	(to) you	te (fam)
you	le (pol)	(to) you	le (pol)
him	le	(to) him	le
her	la	(to) her	le
it	lo	(to) it	le
us	nos	(to) us	nos
you	os (pl fam)	(to) you	os (pl fam)
you	les (pl pol)	(to) you	les (pl pol)
them	les	(to) them	les

Reflexive Pronoun

myself	me
yourself	te (fam)
yourself	se (pol)
himself	se
herself	se
itself	se
ourselves	nos
yourselves	os (pl fam)
yourselves	se (pl pol)
themselves	se

Possessive Pronoun

mine	mío/a
yours	tuyo/a (fam)
yours	suyo/a (pol)
his	suyo/a, suyos/as, de él
hers	suyo/a, suyos/as, de ella
its	suyo/a, suyos/as
ours	nuestro/a, nuestros/as
yours	vuestro/a, vuestros/as (pl fam)
yours	suyo/a, suyos/as (pl pol)
theirs	suyo/a, suyos/as

The gender of a pronoun refers to the gender of the object you are talking about, and not to your own gender. Whether you yourself are male or female, you would say the book (masculine) is mine (*el libro es mío*), or the house (feminine) is mine (*la casa es mía*).

When referring to parts of your body, the possessive pronoun is not used – you would say 'the leg' (*la pierna*) rather than 'my leg' (*mí pierna*)

VERBS
VERBOS

All verbs in their infinitive form end in -ar, -er or -ir. Each verb has a stem or a root and an appropriate ending (be it -ar, -er or -ir). The stem of the verb is the part that precedes the ending. For example, the verb *cantar* (to sing) can be broken up as follows: *cant-* (root) and -*ar* (ending).

The verbs that never change their stem and follow conjugation patterns are called *regulares* (about 75% of verbs), and the ones that change stem are called *irregulares* (about 25%).

Examples of REGULAR verbs, present tense:

AMAR (to love)
yo amO
tú amAS
él/ella/usted amA
nosotros amAMOS
vosotos amÁIS
ellos/ustedes amAN

TEMER (to fear)
yo temO
tú temES
él/ella/usted temE
nosotros temEMOS
vosotros temÉIS
ellos/ustedes temEN

PARTIR (to leave)
yo partO
tú partES
él/ella/usted partE
nosotros partIMOS
vosotros partÍS
ellos/ustedes partEN

Here are some useful IRREGULAR verbs:

TENER (to have)
yo tengo
tú tienes
él/ella/usted tiene
nosotros tenemos
vosotros tenéis
ellos/ustedes tienen

QUERER (to want)
yo quiero
tú quieres
él/ella/usted quiere
nosotros queremos
vosotros queréis
ellos/ustedes quieren

IR (to go)
yo voy
tú vas
él/ella/usted va
nosotros vamos
vosotros vais
ellos/ustedes van

PODER (can)
yo puedo
tú puedes
él/ella/usted puede
nosotros podemos
vosotros podéis
ellos/ustedes pueden

SER (to be)
yo soy
tú eres
él/ella/usted es
nosotros somos
vosotros sois
ellos/ustedes son

ESTAR (to be)
yo estoy
tú estás
él/ella/usted está

ESTAR (continued)
nosotros estamos,
vosotros estáis
ellos/ustedes están

HACER (to make/do)
yo hago
tú haces
él/ella/usted hace
nosotros hacemos
vosotros hacéis
ellos/ustedes hacen

DECIR (to say)
yo digo
tú dices
él/ella/usted dice
nosotros decimos
vosotros decís
ellos/ustedes dicen

NOUNS – SUSTANTIVOS

Nouns ending in -o are usually masculine and nouns ending in -a are usually feminine. To form the plural, add -s if the noun ends in a vowel and -es if the noun ends in a consonant.

ARTICLES – ARTÍCULOS

Definite Article (Artículo Definido) – **the**

el	(masc. sing.)	*la*	(fem. sing.)
los	(masc. pl.)	*las*	(fem. pl.)

Examples:

el libro (the book)   *la casa* (the house)
los libros (the books)   *las casas* (the houses)

Indefinite Article (Artículo Indefinido) – **a, some**

un	(masc. sing.)	*una*	(fem. sing.)
unos	(masc. pl.)	*unas*	(fem. pl.)

Examples:

un perro (a dog)   *una planta* (a plant)
unos perros (some dogs) *unas plantas*
                                          (some plants)

ADJECTIVES – ADJETIVOS

Adjectives usually follow the nouns they qualify
(*un libro nuevo* – a new book). Most adjectives
have a masculine and a feminine form (red –
rojo/roja) as well as a singular and plural form
(red – *rojos/rojas*). All adjectives agree in gender and number with the nouns they qualify.
Adjectives not ending in -o or -a do not change

into the masculine or feminine form, but do
change to form plurals (*la casa grande* – the big
house; *las casas grandes* – the big houses).

PUNCTUATION
PUNTUACIÓN
You may have noticed the upside-down ques-
tions marks and exclamation marks used on
page 12. In Spanish, a question is introduced
by such an upside-down question mark, and
concluded with a 'right-way-up' question mark
as we know it in English. The same is true of
the exclamation mark.

WORD ORDER
ORDEN DE LAS PALABRAS
Spanish word order will probably seem strange
to English ears. The adjective usually comes
after the noun it modifies (see page 20), but
quantifying adjectives usually precede the noun
(many books – *muchos libros*). The adjective
also precedes the noun if you want to empha-
size the adjective rather than the noun.
  A question usually has exactly the same word
order as a statement, but is distinguished from
a statement by the two question marks.

BASICS

NUMBERS
NÚMEROS

0	cero (<u>seh</u>-roh)
1	uno (<u>oo</u>-noh)
2	dos (doss)
3	tres (tress)
4	cuatro (<u>kwat</u>-roh)
5	cinco (<u>seeng</u>-koh)
6	seis (sayss)
7	siete (<u>s'yet</u>-teh)
8	ocho (<u>ot</u>-choh)
9	nueve (<u>nweh</u>-veh)
10	diez (d'yess)
11	once (<u>on</u>-seh)
12	doce (<u>doh</u>-seh)
13	trece (<u>treh</u>-seh)
14	catorce (kah-<u>torr</u>-seh)
15	quince (<u>keen</u>-seh)
16	dieciséis (d'yes-ee-<u>sayss</u>)
17	diecisiete (d'yes-ee-<u>s'yet</u>-teh)
18	dieciocho (d'yes-ee-<u>ot</u>-choh)
19	diecinueve (d'yes-ee-<u>nweh</u>-veh)
20	veinte (<u>bayn</u>-teh)
21	veintiuno (<u>bayn</u>-tee-<u>oo</u>-noh)
22	veintidós (bayn-tee-<u>doss</u>)
30	treinta (<u>trayn</u>-ta)
31	treinta y uno (<u>trayn</u>-ta-ee-<u>oo</u>-noh)
40	cuarenta (kwa-<u>ren</u>-ta)
50	cincuenta (seeng-<u>kwen</u>-ta)
60	sesenta (seh-<u>sen</u>-ta)
70	setenta (seh-<u>ten</u>-ta)
80	ochenta (otch-<u>en</u>-ta)
90	noventa (noh-<u>ven</u>-ta)
100	cien (s'yen)
101	ciento uno (<u>s'yen</u>-toh-<u>oo</u>-noh)
120	ciento viente (<u>s'yen</u>-toh-<u>bayn</u>-teh)
200	doscientos (doss-<u>s'yen</u>-toss)
500	quinientos (keen-<u>yen</u>-toss)
1000	mil (meel)
1 million	un millón (oon mee-<u>yon</u>)
1 billion	un billón (oon bee-<u>yon</u>)

DAYS DÍAS	**MONTHS** MESES

Monday
lunes (*loo*-ness)

Tuesday
martes (*marr*-tess)

Wednesday
miércoles
(*m'yehr*-koh-less)

Thursday
jueves (*khweh*-vess)

Friday
viernes (*b'yer*-ness)

Saturday
sábado (*sabba*-doh)

Sunday
domingo
(doh-*meeng*-goh)

weekdays
días de semana (*dee*-yass deh seh-*ma*-na)

weekends
fines de semana (*fee*-ness deh seh-*ma*-na)

public holidays
feriados (ferr-*ya*-doss)

January
enero (eh-*neh*-roh)

February
febrero (feb-*reh*-roh)

March
marzo (*marr*-soh)

April
abril (ab-*reel*)

May
mayo (*ma*-yoh)

June
junio (*khoon*-yoh)

July
julio (*khool*-yoh)

August
agosto (a*goss*-toh)

September
setiembre (set-*yem*-breh)

October
octubre (ok-*too*-breh)

November
noviembre
(nov-*yem*-breh)

December
diciembre
(dees-_yem_-breh)

TIME
LA HORA
---

in the morning
por la mañana
(porr la man-_ya_-na)

in the afternoon
por la tarde
(porr la _tarr_-deh)

in the evening
por la noche
(por la _not_che)

What is the time?
¿Qué hora es?
(keh _oh_-ra ess)

* **it's one o'clock**
* es la una (ess la _oo_-na)

* **it's quarter to three**
* son cuarto para las tres
(son _kwarr_-toh parra
lass _tress_)

* **it's half past two**
* son las dos y media
(son lass _doss_ ee
med-ya)

* **twenty past two**
* son las dos y veinte
(son lass doss ee
bayn-teh)

* **early**
* temprano (tem-_pra_-noh)

* **late**
* tarde (_tarr_-deh)

at 10 a.m. (10:00)
a las diez de la mañana
(allas _d'yess_ della
man-_ya_-na)

at 5 p.m. (17:00)
a las cinco de la tarde
(allas _seeng_-koh della
tarr-deh)

at 9 p.m. (21:00)
a las nueve de la noche
(allas _nweh_-veh della
notcheh)

day after tomorrow
pasado mañana
(pa-_saa_-doh man-_ya_-na)

day before yesterday
anteayer (anteh-a-_yerr_)

this morning
esta mañana
(_ess_-ta man-_ya_-na)

yesterday evening
ayer por la noche/tarde
(a-_yerr_ porr la _no_tcheh/
tarr-deh)

tomorrow morning
mañana por la mañana
(man-_ya_-na porr la
man-_ya_-na)

last night
anoche (a-_no_tcheh)

this week
esta semana
(ess-ta seh-_ma_-na)

next week
la semana próxima
(la seh-_ma_-na
prok-see-ma)

now
ahora (a-_oh_-ra)

What is today's date?
¿Qué día es?
(keh _dee_-ya ess)
¿Qué día es hoy?
(keh _dee_-ya ess _oy_)

It's 4 June
Es el cuatro de junio
(ess ell _kwat_-roh de
khoon-yoh)

| GREETINGS |
| SALUDOS |

Good morning
Buenos días
(_bwenn_oss _dee_-yass)

Good afternoon
Buenas tardes
(_bwenn_ass _tarr_-dess)

Good evening
Buenas tardes/noches
(_bwenn_ass _tarr_-dess/
_no_tchess)

Good night
Buenas noches
(_bwenn_ass _no_tchess)

Hello
Hola (_Olla_)

Goodbye
Adiós (ad-_yoss_)

Cheerio
Chau (chow)

See you soon
Hasta pronto
(_ass_-ta _pron_-toh)

See you later
Hasta luego
(_ass_-ta _lwe_-goh)

Have a good time
Que se divierta/que la pase bien *(keh seh deev-yehr-ta/ keh la passeh byen)*

I have to go now
Debo irme ahora *(deb-boh eer-meh a-oh-ra)*

It was very nice
Fue muy agradable *(fweh mooee agra-da-bleh)*

My name is ...
Mi nombre es ... *(mee nom-breh ess ...)*

What is your name?
¿Cómo se llama? (pol) *(kom-moh seh yaa-ma)*
¿Cómo te llamas? (fam) *(kom-moh teh yaa-mass)*

Pleased to meet you!
¡Mucho gusto! *(moo-choh goos-toh)*

How are you?
¿Cómo está? (pol) *(kom-moh ess-ta)*
¿Que tal? (fam) *(keh tal)*

Fine, thanks. And you?
Bien, gracias. ¿Y usted? (pol) *(byen graas-yass, ee oos-ted)*

GENERAL
GENERALES

Do you speak English?
¿Habla inglés? *(ab-la eeng-gless)*

I don't understand
No comprendo/ no entiendo *(noh kom-pren-doh/noh ent-yen-doh)*

Please speak slowly
Por favor, hable despacio *(por fa-vor, ab-leh des-pa-s'yoh)*

Please repeat that
Por favor, repita eso *(por fa-vor, reh-pee-ta essoh)*

Please write it down
Por favor, escríbalo *(por fa-vor, es-cree-ba-loh)*

Excuse me please
Discúlpeme/perdóneme *(dees-cool-peh-meh/ per-donneh-meh)*

Could you help me?
¿Me puede ayudar? *(meh pweh-deh a-yoo-darr)*

Okay, very well
Pura vida *(poo-ra bee-da)*

Could you do me a favour?
¿Puede hacerme un favor? *(pweh-deh a-serr-meh oon fa-vor)*

Can you show me?
¿Puede mostrarme? *(pweh-deh moss-trarr-meh)*

how?
¿cómo? *(kom-moh)*

where?
¿dónde? *(donn-deh)*

when?
¿cuándo? *(kwan-doh)*

who?
¿quién? *(k'yen)*

why?
¿por qué? *(porr keh)*

which?
¿cuál? *(kwal)*

I need ...
necesito ...
(ne-seh-see-toh ...)

yes, no
sí, no *(see, noh)*

FORMS & SIGNS
IMPRESOS & SIGNOS

Please complete in block letters
Rellene con mayúsculas de imprenta, por favor *(reh-yen-neh con ma-yoos-cool-las deh eem-pren-ta, por fa-vor)*

Surname
Apellido *(appeh-yee-doh)*

First names
Nombres *(nom-bress)*

Date of birth
Fecha de nacimiento *(fetcha deh nasee-m'yen-toh)*

Place of birth
Lugar de nacimiento *(loo-garr deh nasee-m'yen-toh)*

Occupation
Profesión *(proh-fes-s'yon)*

Nationality
Nacionalidad *(na-s'yoh-nalli-dad)*

Address
Dirección *(dee-rec-s'yon)*

Date of arrival
Fecha de llegada (*fetcha deh yeg-ga-da*)

Date of departure
Fecha de partida (*fetcha deh parr-tee-dah*)

Passport number
Número de pasaporte (*noo-meh-roh deh passa-por-teh*)

I.D. number
Número de documento de identidad (*noo-meh-roh deh dok-oo-men-toh deh ee-dentee-dad*)

Issued at
Expedido en (*expeh-dee-doh en*)

Engaged, Vacant
Ocupado, Libre (*okkoo-pa-doh, lee-breh*)

No trespassing
No pasar (*noh pas-sarr*)

Out of order
No funciona (*noh foon-s'yoh-na*)

Please don't disturb
Por favor, no moleste (*por fa-vor, noh moh-less-teh*)

Push, Pull
Empuje, Tire (*em-poo-kheh, tee-reh*)

Adults and children
Adultos y niños (*a-dool-toss ee neen-yoss*)

Lift/Elevator
Ascensor/Elevador (*as-senn-sorr/ele-va-dorr*)

Escalator
Escalera mecánica (*es-ca-leh-ra meh-ka-nee-ka*)

Wet paint
Pintura fresca (*peen-too-ra fress-ka*)

Open, Closed
Abierto, Cerrado (*ab'yer-toh, ser-ra-doh*)

Till/Cash Desk
Caja (*ka-kha*)

Opening hours
Horario de trabajo (*or-raar-yoh deh tra-ba-khoh*)

Self-service
Autoservicio (*aoo-toh-serr-vee-s'yoh*)

Waiting Room
Sala de espera (*sa-la deh ess-peh-rah*)

BUS/TRAM STOP
PARADA DE AUTOBÚS/TRANVÍA

Where is the bus/tram stop?
¿Dónde está la parada de autobús/tranvía?
(Donn-deh ess-ta la pa-ra-da deh aoo-toh-booss/tram-bee-ya)

Which bus do I take?
¿Cuál autobús debo tomar? *(Kwal aoo-toh-booss debboh toh-marr)*

How often do the buses go?
¿Con qué frecuencia pasan los buses? *(Kon keh freh-kwens-ya pas-san loss booss-ess)*

When is the last bus?
¿A qué hora pasa el ultimo autobús? *(A keh oh-ra passa ell ool-tee-moh aoo-toh-booss)*

Which ticket must I buy?
¿Cuál tiquete debo comprar? *(Kwal tee-ket-teh debboh kom-prarr)*

Where must I go?
¿Dónde debo ir?
(Donn-deh debboh eer)

I want to go to ....
Quiero ir a...
(K'yeh-roh eer a ...)

What is the fare to...?
¿Cuánto cuesta a ...?
(Kwan-toh kwess-ta a ...)

When is the next bus?
¿En cuánto tiempo llegará el próximo Autobús?
(En kwan-toh t'yem-poh yegga-ra ell prok-see-moh aoo-toh-booss)

UNDERGROUND/ SUBWAY/METRO
METRO/ SUBTERRÁNEO

entrance, exit
entrada, salida
(en-tra-da, sa-lee-da)

inner zone, outer zone
zona interna, zona externa
(soh-na een-terr-na, soh-na ex-terr-na)

Where is the underground/subway station?
¿Dónde está la estación de metro? (*Donn*-deh ess-*ta* la es-ta-s'*yon* deh *met*-roh)

Do you have a map for the metro?
¿Tiene un mapa para el metro? (*T'yen*-neh oon *mappa* parra ell *met*-roh)

I want to go to ....
Quiero ir a...
(K'*yeh*-roh eer a ...)

Can you give me change?
¿Puede cambiarme/darme cambio? (*Pweh*-deh kam-b'*yarr*-meh/*darr*-meh kam-b'yoh)

Which ticket must I buy?
¿Cuál tiquete debo comprar? (Kwal tee-*ket*-teh *debb*oh kom-*prarr*)

When is the next train?
¿En cuánto tiempo llegará el próximo tren? (En *kwan*-toh t'*yem*-poh yegga-*ra* ell *prok*-see-moh *trenn*)

TRAIN/RAILWAY
TREN/FERROCARRIL

Where is the railway station?
¿Dónde está la estación de tren? (*Donn*-deh ess-*ta* la es-ta-s'*yon* deh *trenn*)

departure
salidas (sa-*lee*-dass)

arrival
llegadas (yeg-*ga*-dass)

Which platform?
¿Cuál plataforma? (*Kwal* platta-*for*-ma)

Do you have a timetable?
¿Tiene un horario? (T'*yen*-neh oon or-*raar*-yoh)

A ... ticket please
Un tiquete ... por favor (Oon tee-*ket*-teh ... por fa-*vor*)

- ◆ **single**
- ◆ ida (*ee*-da)

- ◆ **return**
- ◆ ida y vuelta (*ee*-da ee *bwel*-ta)

◆ **child's**
◆ infantil *(een-fan-teel)*

◆ **first class**
◆ primera clase
  (pree-meh-ra kla-seh)

◆ **second class**
◆ segunda clase
  (seh-goon-da kla-seh)

◆ **smoking**
◆ fumador *(foo-ma-dorr)*

◆ **non-smoking**
◆ no fumador *(noh
  foo-ma-dorr)*

**Do I have to pay a
supplement?**
¿Debo pagar exceso?
*(Debboh pa-garr
ex-sessoh*

**Is my ticket valid on
this train?**
¿Mi tiquete es válido en
este tren? *(Mee tee-ket-
teh ess ba-lee-doh en
ess-teh trenn)*

**Where do I have to
get off?**
¿Dónde debo bajarme?
*(Donn-deh debboh
ba-khar-meh)*

I want to book ...
Quiero reservar ...
(K'yeh-roh reh-ser-varr ...)

◆ **a seat**
◆ un asiento
  (oon ass-yen-toh)

◆ **a couchette**
◆ un coche cama
  (oon kotcheh ca-ma)

Is this seat free?
¿Este asiento está
ocupado? *(Ess-teh
ass-yen-toh ess-ta
okkoo-pa-doh)*

That is my seat
Ese es mi asiento
*(Es-seh ess mee
ass-yen-toh)*

**May I open (close)
the window?**
¿Puedo abrir (cerrar) la
ventana? *(Pweh-doh
ab-reer [ser-rarr] la
ben-ta-na)*

**Where is the
restaurant car?**
¿Dónde está el coche
comedor? *(Donn-deh
ess-ta ell kotcheh
kommeh-dorr)*

Is there a sleeper?
¿Hay una coche cama?
*(Aee oo-na kotcheh
ca-ma)*

EC – Eurocity
International express,
supplement payable

IC – Intercity
Luxury international
express, supplement
payable

stationmaster
jefe de estación *(khef-feh
deh ess-ta-s'yon)*

BOATS
BARCOS

---

cruise
crucero *(kroo-seh-roh)*

Can we hire a boat?
¿Podemos alquilar un
barco/bote? *(Poh-deh-
moss al-kee-larr oon
barr-koh/boh-teh)*

**How much is a
round trip?**
¿Cuánto cuesta un viaje
de ida y vuelta?
*(Kwan-toh kwes-ta oon
b'ya-kheh deh ee-da ee
bwel-ta)*

one ticket
un tiquete
(oon tee-ket-teh)

two tickets
dos tiquetes
(doss tee-ket-tess)

**Can we eat on
board?**
¿Se puede comer a
bordo? *(Seh pweh-deh
ko-merr a borr-doh)*

**When is the last
boat?**
¿A qué hora sale el último
barco? *(A keh oh-ra sa-leh
ell ool-tee-moh barr-koh)*

**When is the next
ferry?**
¿A qué hora sale la
próxima barca/
transbordador?
*(A keh oh-ra sa-leh la
prok-see-ma barr-ka/
trans-borda-dorr)*

**How long does the
crossing take?**
¿Cuánto tarda el cruce?
*(Kwan-toh tarr-da ell
kroo-seh)*

Is the sea rough?
¿El mar está bravo?
(Ell marr ess-ta bra-voh)

TAXI
TAXI

Please order me a taxi
Por favor, llame un taxi *(Por fa-vor, ya-meh oon taxi)*

Where can I get a taxi?
¿Dónde puedo coger/tomar un taxi?
(Donn-deh pweh-doh ko-kherr/toh-marr oon taxi)

To this address, please
A esta dirección, por favor *(A ess-ta dee-reks-s'yon, por fa-vor)*

How much is it to the centre?
¿Cuánto cuesta al centro de la ciudad?*(Kwan-toh kwess-ta al sen-troh della see-oo-dad)*

To the airport, please
Al aeropuerto, por favor *(Al a-ehroh-pwerr-toh, por fa-vor)*

To the station, please
A la estación, por favor *(Alla es-ta-s'yon por fa-vor)*

Keep the change
Quédese con el cambio *(Keh-deh-seh kon ell kam-b'yoh)*

I need a receipt
Necesito un recibo *(Ne-seh-see-toh oon reh-see-boh*

AIRPORT
AEROPUERTO

arrival
llegadas *(yeg-ga-dass)*

departure
salidas *(sa-lee-dass)*

flight number
número de vuelo *(noo-meh-roh deh bweh-loh)*

delay
retraso *(re-tra-soh)*

check-in
facturación de equipages *(fak-too-ra-s'yon deh ekkee-pa-khess)*

hand luggage
equipaje de mano *(ekkee-pa-khe deh ma-noh)*

boarding card
tarjeta de embarque
*(tarr-kheh-ta deh
em-barr-keh)*

gate
puerta *(pwerr-ta)*

valid, invalid
válido, inválido *(ba-lee-doh, eem-ba-lee-doh)*

baggage/luggage claim
recolección de equipajes
*(rekko-lek-s'yon deh
ekkee-pa-khess)*

lost property office
oficina de objetos
perdidos *(offee-see-na
deh ob-khe-toss perr-dee-doss)*

Where do I get the bus to the centre?
¿Dónde cojo/tomo el
autobús a la ciudad?
*(Donn-deh koh-khoh/
toh-moh ell aoo-toh-booss alla see-oo-dad)*

Where do I check in for ...?
¿Dónde está el mostrador
de ...? *(Donn-deh ess-ta
ell moss-tra-dorr deh ...)*

An aisle/window seat, please
Un asiento en pasillo/
ventanilla, por favor
*(Oon ass-yen-toh en
pa-see-yoh/benta-nee-ya,
por fa-vor)*

Where is the gate for the flight to ....?
¿Dónde está la puerta
de embarque para el
vuelo ...? *(Donn-deh
ess-ta la pwerr-ta deh
em-barr-keh parra ell
bweh-loh ...)*

I have nothing to declare
Nada que declarar
(Na-da keh dekla-rarr)

It's for my own personal use
Es de uso personal *(Ess
deh oo-soh perr-soh-nal)*

The flight has been cancelled
El vuelo ha sido cancelado
*(Ell bweh-loh a see-doh
kan-seh-la-doh)*

The flight has been delayed
El vuelo ha sido demorado
*(Ell bweh-loh a see-doh
demoh-ra-doh)*

ROAD TRAVEL/ CAR HIRE
VIAJE EN CARRETERA/ ALQUILER DE VEHÍCULOS

Have you got a road map?
¿Tiene un mapa de carreteras? *(T'yen-neh oon mappa deh karreh-teh-rass)*

How many kilometres is it to ...?
¿Cuántos kilómetros hay a ...? *(Kwan-toss kee-lommeh-tross aee a ...)*

Where is the nearest garage?
¿Dónde está la estación de servicio más cercana? *(Donn-deh ess-ta la esta-s'yon deh serr-vees-yo mahss ser-ka-na)*

Fill it up, please
Llene el tanque, por favor *(Yen-neh ell tan-keh, por fa-vor)*

Please check the oil, water, battery, tyres
Por favor, revise el aceite, el agua, la batería, las llantas *(Por fa-vor, reh-vee-seh ell asay-teh, ell agwa, la ba-teh-ree-ya, lass yann-tass)*

I'd like to hire a car
Quiero alquilar un carro/ auto *(K'yeh-roh al-kee-larr oon karr-roh/aoo-toh)*

How much does it cost per day/week?
¿Cuánto cuesta por día/ semana? *(Kwan-toh kwess-ta porr dee-ya/ seh-ma-na)*

What do you charge per kilometre?
¿Cuánto cobran por kiló- metro? *(Kwan-toh kob-ran porr kee-lommeh-troh)*

Is mileage unlimited?
¿El kilometraje es ilimitado? *(Ell kee-lommeh-tra-kheh ess ee-leemee-ta-doh)*

Where can I pick up the car?
¿Dónde recojo el carro/ auto? *(Donn-deh reh-koh-khoh ell karr-roh/aoo-toh)*

Where can I leave the car?
¿Dónde puedo dejar el carro/auto? *(Donn-deh pweh-doh deh-kharr ell karr-roh/aoo-toh)*

garage
gasolinera/estación de servicio (ga-soh-lee-_neh_-ra/ess-ta-s'_yon_ deh serr-_vees_-yo)

headlight
faro (_fa_-roh)

windscreen
parabrisas (parra-_bree_-sass)

indicator
intermitente (een-termee-_ten_-teh)

What is the speed limit?
¿Cuál es el límite de velocidad? (Kwal ess ell _lee_-mee-teh deh beh-loh-see-_dad_)

The keys are locked in the car
Las llaves están dentro del carro/auto cerrado (Lass _ya_-vess ess-_tann den_-troh dell _karr_-roh/_aoo_-toh ser-_ra_-doh)

The engine is overheating
El motor está recalentado (Ell moh-_torr_ ess-_ta_ reh-kallen-_ta_-doh)

Have you got ...?
Tiene ...? (T'_yen_-neh ...)

◆ **a towing rope**
◆ una cuerda de remolque (oona _kwerr_-da deh reh-_moll_-keh)

◆ **a spanner**
◆ una llave de tuercas (oona _ya_-veh deh _twerr_-kass)

◆ **a screwdriver**
◆ un destornillador (oon dess-tornee-ya-_dorr_)

ROAD SIGNS
SEÑALES DE TRÁFICO

No through road
No pasar (Noh pas-_sarr_)

one-way street
calle de una sola vía (_ka_-yeh deh oona _soll_a _bee_-ya)

entrance
entrada (en-_tra_-da)

exit
salida (sa-_lee_-da)

danger
peligro (peh-_lee_-groh)

pedestrians
peatones
(peh-ya-<u>toh</u>-ness)

Keep entrance clear
No bloquear la entrada
(Noh bloh-keh-<u>yarr</u> la
en-<u>tra</u>-da)

Residents only
Sólo para residentes
(<u>Solloh</u> parra reh-see-
<u>den</u>-tess)

speed limit
límite de velocidad
(lee-mee-teh deh
beh-loh-see-<u>dad</u>)

stop
pare (<u>pa</u>-reh)

No entry
Prohibida la entrada (Pro-
ee-<u>bee</u>-da la en-<u>tra</u>-da)

roundabout
rotonda (roh-<u>ton</u>-da)

Insert coins
Ponga menudo/monedas
(<u>Pong</u>-ga meh-<u>noo</u>-doh/
moh-<u>neh</u>-dass)

No Parking
Prohibido estacionar
(Pro-ee-<u>bee</u>-doh
es-ta-s'yoh-<u>narr</u>

parking garage
zona de estacionamiento
(<u>soh</u>-na deh ess-ta-
s'yon-na-m'<u>yen</u>-toh)

supervised car park
estacionamiento
controlado (ess-ta-s'yon-
na-m'<u>yen</u>-toh kon-troh-
<u>la</u>-doh)

No right turn
Prohibido girar a la
derecha (pro-ee-<u>bee</u>-doh
khee-<u>rarr</u> alla deh-<u>ret</u>cha)

cul de sac
calle sin salida (<u>ka</u>-yeh
seen sa-<u>lee</u>-da)

roadworks
trabajos en la vía
(tra-<u>ba</u>-khoss en la
<u>bee</u>-ya)

detour
desvío (dess-<u>vee</u>-oh)

Caution
Cuidado (Kwee-<u>da</u>-doh)

uneven surface
calzada irregular (kal-<u>sa</u>-da
ee-reh-goo-<u>larr</u>)

toll
peaje (peh-<u>a</u>-kheh)

ACCOMMODATION
ALOJAMIENTO

bed & breakfast
pensión *(pen-s'yon)*

vacancies
habitación libre *(abbee-ta-s'yon lee-breh)*

Have you a room ...?
¿Tiene una habitación ...?
(T'yenn-neh oona abbee-ta-s'yon)

♦ **for tonight**
♦ para esta noche
  (parra ess-ta notcheh)

♦ **with breakfast**
♦ con desayuno *(kon dessa-yoo-noh)*

♦ **with bath**
♦ con baño *(kon banyo)*

♦ **with shower**
♦ con ducha *(kon dootcha)*

♦ **a single room**
♦ habitación sencilla/para una persona *(abbee-ta-s'yon sen-see-ya/parra oona per-soh-na)*

♦ **a double room**
♦ habitación doble
  (abbee-ta-s'yon dob-bleh)

♦ **a family room**
♦ habitación familiar
  (abbee-ta-s'yon fa-meel-yar)

How much is the room ...?
¿Cuánto cuesta la habitación ...?
(Kwan-toh kwess-ta la abbee-ta-s'yon)

♦ **per day/week**
♦ por día/semana *(por dee-ya/se-ma-na)*

Have you got anything cheaper/better?
¿Hay algo mejor/más barato? *(Aee al-goh meh-khorr/mahss ba-ra-toh)*

May I see the room?
¿Puedo ver la habitación? *(Pweh-doh berr la abbee-ta-s'yon)*

Do you have a cot?
¿Tiene una cuna?
(T'yenn-neh oona koo-na)

What time is breakfast/dinner?
¿A qué hora es el desayuno/la cena? (A keh oh-ra ess ell dessa-yoo-noh/la seh-na)

room service
el servicio de cuarto/habitaciones (ell serr-vee-s'yoh deh kwarr-toh/abbee-ta-s'yon-ness)

Please bring ...
Por favor trae/traiga ... (Por fa-vor tra-eh/traee-ga)

◆ toilet paper
◆ papel higiénico (pa-pell ee-khee-en-ee-koh)

◆ clean towels
◆ toallas limpias (toh-ay-yas leem-p'yass)

Please clean the bath
Por favor limpie la bañera (Por fa-vor leem-p'yeh la ban-yeh-ra)

Please put fresh sheets on the bed
Por favor, cambie las sábanas (Por fa-vor, kam-b'yeh lass sa-ba-nass)

Please don't touch ...
Por favor, no toque ... (Por fa-vor, noh tok-keh)

◆ my briefcase
◆ mi maletín (mee ma-leh-teen)

◆ my laptop
◆ mi computadora/computador portátil (mee kom-poo-ta-doh-ra/kom-poo-ta-dorr porr-ta-teel)

My ... doesn't work
Mi ... no funciona (Mee ... noh foon-s'yoh-na)

◆ toilet
◆ inodoro/servicio (eeno-doh-roh/serr-vee-s'yoh

◆ bedside lamp
◆ lámpara (lam-pa-ra)

◆ air conditioning
◆ aire acondicionado (aee-reh akon-dee-s'yoh-na-doh

There is no hot water
No hay agua caliente (Noh aee agwa kallee-yen-teh)

RECEPTION
RECEPCIÓN

Are there any messages for me?
¿Hay algún mensaje para mí? (_Aee_ al-_goon_ men-_sa_-kheh parra _mee_)

Has anyone asked for me?
¿Alguien ha preguntado por mí? (_Al_-ghee-en a pre-goon-_ta_-doh porr _mee_)

Can I leave a message for someone?
¿Puedo dejar un mensaje para alguien? (_Pweh_-doh deh-_kharr_ oon men-_sa_-kheh parra _al_-ghee-en)

Is there a laundry service?
¿Hay servicio de lavandería? (_Aee_ serr-_vee_-s'yoh de la-van-deh-_ree_-ya)

I need a wake-up call at 7 o'clock
¿Puede despertarme a las 7 en punto? (_Pweh_-deh des-per-_tarr_-meh a lass s'_yet_-teh en _poon_-toh)

What number must I dial for room service?
¿Cuál es el número de servicio de cuarto? (_Kwal_ ess ell _noo_-meh-roh deh serr-_vee_-s'yoh deh _kwarr_-toh)

Where is the lift/elevator?
¿Dónde está el ascensor? (_Donn_-deh ess-_ta_ ell as-sen-_sorr_)

Do you arrange tours?
¿Organiza los viajes? (Orr-ga-_nee_-sa loss b'_ya_-khess)

Please prepare the bill
Por favor, prepare la cuenta (Por fa-_vor_, preh-_parreh_ la _kwen_-ta)

There is a mistake in this bill
Hay un error en esta cuenta (_Aee_ oon err_or_ en _ess_-ta _kwen_-ta)

I'm leaving tomorrow
Salgo mañana (_Sall_-goh man-_ya_-na)

SELF-CATERING
ALOJAMIENTO CON
COCINA PROPIA

Have you any vacancies?
¿Hay lugar? (*Aee* loo-*garr*)

How much is it per night/week?
¿Cuánto cuesta por noche/semana?
(*Kwan*-toh *kwess*-ta porr *notch*eh)

How big is it?
¿Cuál es el tamaño?
(*Kwal* ess ell ta-*man*-yoh)

Do you allow children?
¿Se permiten niños? (Seh per-*mee*-ten *neen*-yoss)

Please, show me how ... works
Por favor, enséñeme cómo ... funciona (Por fa-*vor*, en-*sen*-yemmeh *kom*-moh ... foon-s'*yoh*-na)

◆ **the cooker/stove/ oven**
◆ la cocina/horno
(la koh-*see*-na/*orr*-noh)

◆ **the washing machine**
◆ la lavadora
(la lava-*doh*-ra)

◆ **the dryer**
◆ la secadora
(la se-ka-*doh*-ra)

◆ **the hair-dryer**
◆ el secador de pelo
(ell se-ka-*dorr* deh *peh*-loh)

◆ **the heater**
◆ el calefactor
(ell ka-leh-fak-*torr*)

◆ **the water heater**
◆ el calentador para agua
(ell ka-lenta-*dorr* parra *agwa*)

Where is/are ...?
¿Dónde está/están ...?
(*Donn*-deh ess-*ta*/ ess-*tan* ...)

◆ **the keys**
◆ las llaves (lass *ya*-vess)

◆ **the switch**
◆ el interruptor
(ell een-ter-roop-*torr*)

◆ **the fuses**
◆ los fusibles
(loss foo-*see*-bless)

Is there ...?
¿Hay ...? *(Aee ...)*

♦ **a cot**
♦ una cuna? *(oona koo-na)*

♦ **a high chair**
♦ una silla alta para niños *(oona see-ya alta parra neen-yoss)*

♦ **a safe**
♦ una caja de seguridad *(oona ka-kha deh seh-goo-ree-dad)*

We need more ...
necesitamos más ... *(ne-seh-see-ta-moss mahss)*

♦ **cutlery**
♦ cubertería *(koo-ber-teh-ree-ya)*

♦ **crockery**
♦ vajilla *(ba-khee-ya)*

♦ **sheets**
♦ sábanas *(sa-ba-nass)*

♦ **blankets**
♦ cobertores *(kobber-toh-ress)*

♦ **pillows**
♦ almohadas *(al-moh-aa-dass)*

Is there ... in the vicinity?
¿Hay ... en el barrio? *(Aee ... en ell barr-yo)*

♦ **a shop**
♦ una tienda *(oona t'yen-da)*

♦ **a restaurant**
♦ un restaurante *(oon resta-oo-ran-teh)*

♦ **a bus/tram**
♦ un autobús/tranvía *(oon aoo-toh-booss/ tram-bee-ya)*

We'd like to stay for three nights/a week
Nos gustaría quedarnos por tres noches/una semana *(Nos goos-ta-ree-ya keh-darr-nos porr tress notchess/oona seh-ma-na)*

I have locked myself out
No puedo entrar *(No pweh-doh en-trar)*

The window won't open/close
La ventana no abre/cierra *(La ben-ta-na noh ab-reh/s'yer-ra)*

CAMPING
ACAMPAR

caravan
casa rodante/
autocaravana
*(ka-sa roh-dan-teh/
aoo-toh-karra-va-na)*

**Have you got a list
of campsites?**
¿Tiene una lista de sitios
para acampar? *(T'yen-neh
oona lees-ta deh seet-
yoss parra a-kam-parr)*

**Are there any sites
available?**
¿Hay sitios disponibles?
*(Aee seet-yoss
dees-poh-nee-bless)*

**How much is it
per night/week?**
¿Cuánto cuesta por
noche/semana?
*(Kwan-toh kwess-ta
porr notcheh)*

**Can we park the
caravan here?**
¿Podemos estacionar la
casa rodante aquí?
*(Poh-deh-moss es-ta-
s'yoh-narr la ka-sa roh-
dan-teh a-kee)*

**Can we camp here
overnight?**
¿Podemos acampar aquí
por la noche? *(Poh-deh-
moss a-kam-parr a-kee
porr la notcheh)*

**This site is very
muddy**
Este sitio está muy
enlodado *(Ess-te
seet-yo ess-ta moo-ee
en-loh-da-doh)*

**Is there a sheltered
site?**
¿Hay un sitio más
protegido? *(Aee oon
seet-yo mahss
pro-teh-khee-doh)*

**Do you have
electricity?**
¿Tienen electricidad?
*(T'yen-nen
elek-tree-see-dad)*

**Is there ... in the
vicinity?**
¿Hay ... en la vecindad?
*(Aee ... en la beh-seen-
dad)*

◆ **a shop**
◆ una tienda
(oona t'yen-da)

◆ **a restaurant**
◆ un restaurante *(oon resta-oo-ran-teh)*

◆ **an eating place**
◆ un lugar para comer *(oon loo-garr parra ko-merr)*

◆ **a garage**
◆ una gasolinera *(oona gassoh-lee-neh-ra)*

We'd like to stay for three nights/a week
Nos gustaría quedarnos por tres noches/una semana *(Nos goos-ta-ree-ya keh-darr-nos porr tress notchess/oona seh-ma-na)*

Is there drinking water?
¿Hay agua potable? *(Aee agwa poh-ta-bleh)*

Can I light a fire here?
¿Puedo encender fuego aquí? *(Pweh-doh en-sen-derr fweh-goh a-kee)*

I'd like to buy fire wood
Me gustaría comprar leña *(Meh goos-ta-ree-a kom-prarr lehn-ya)*

Is the wood dry?
¿Está seca la leña? *(Ess-ta seh-ka la lehn-ya)*

Do you have ... for rent?
¿Tienen ... para alquilar? *(T'yen-nen ... parra al-kee-larr)*

◆ **a tent**
◆ una tienda *(oona t'yen-da)*

◆ **a gas cylinder**
◆ un cilindro de gas *(oon see-leen-droh de gass)*

◆ **a groundsheet**
◆ un aislante para el suelo *(oon aees-lan-teh parra ell sweh-loh)*

Where is/are the nearest ...?
¿Dónde está/están ... más cercano? *(Donn-deh ess-ta/ess-tan ... mahss serr-ka-noh)*

◆ **toilets**
◆ los servicios *(loss serr-vee-s'yoss)*

◆ **sink (for dishes)**
◆ fregadero *(fregga-deh-roh)*

CUTLERY
CUBERTERÍA

knife
cuchillo *(koo-chee-yoh)*

fork, cake fork
tenedor, tenedor de torta
(ten-eh-dorr, ten-eh-dorr deh torr-ta)

spoon, teaspoon
cuchara, cucharilla *(koo-cha-ra, koo-cha-ree-ya)*

crockery
vajilla *(ba-khee-ya)*

plate
plato *(pla-toh)*

cup and saucer, mug
taza y platillo, taza
(ta-sa ee pla-tee-yo, ta-sa)

BREAKFAST
DESAYUNO

coffee
café *(ka-feh)*

◆ **black**
◆ solo *(solloh)*

◆ **with milk, cream**
◆ con leche, crema
(kon letcheh, kreh-ma)

◆ **without sugar**
◆ sin azúcar *(seen a-soo-karr)*

tea
té *(teh)*

◆ **with milk, lemon**
◆ con leche, limón *(kon letcheh, lee-mon)*

bread
pan *(pan)*

rolls
panecillos
(pa-neh-see-yoss)

egg(s)
huevo(s) *(ooweh-voss)*

◆ **boiled – soft, hard**
◆ pasados por agua –
ligeros, duros
(pas-sa-doss porr agwa – lee-khe-ross, doo-ross)

◆ **fried**
◆ fritos *(free-toss)*

◆ **scrambled**
◆ revueltos *(rev-wel-toss)*

◆ poached
◆ escalfados
(es-kal-*fa*-doss)

◆ bacon and eggs
◆ tocino y huevos
(toh-*see*-noh ee
oo*weh*-voss)

cereal
cereal (seh-reh-*al*)

hot milk, cold milk
leche caliente, leche fría
(*let*cheh kall-*yen*-teh,
*let*cheh *free*-ya)

fruit
fruta (*froo*-ta)

orange juice
zumo/jugo de naranja
(*soo*-moh/*khoo*-goh deh
na-*ran*-kha)

jam
jalea/mermelada
(kha-*leh*-a/mer-meh-*la*-da)

marmalade
mermelada
(mer-meh-*la*-da)

pepper
pimienta (peem-*yen*-ta)

salt
sal (*sal*)

LUNCH/DINNER
ALMUERZO/
COMIDA/CENA

**Could we have a
table ...?**
¿Tiene una mesa ...?
(T'*yen*-neh oona *meh*-sa)

◆ by the window
◆ junto a la ventana
(*khoon*-toh alla
ben-*ta*-na)

◆ outside
◆ fuera (*fweh*-ra)

◆ inside
◆ dentro (*den*-troh)

May I have ... ?
¿Puedo ordenar ... ?
(*Pweh*-doh or-deh-*narr*)

◆ the wine list
◆ la carta de vinos (la
karr-ta deh *bee*-noss)

◆ the menu of the day
◆ el menú del día (ell
meh-*noo* dell *dee*-ya)

◆ starters
◆ entrada/primero
(en-*tra*-da/pree-*meh*-roh

- **main course**
- plato principal/segundo *(pla-toh preen-see-pal/ seh-goon-doh)*

- **dessert**
- postre *(poss-treh)*

- **the menu**
- el menú *(ell meh-noo)*

I'll take the set menu
Comeré el menú fijo *(Ko-meh-reh ell meh-noo fee-khoh)*

What is this?
¿Qué es ésto? *(Keh ess ess-toh)*

That is not what I ordered
Esto no es lo que he ordenado *(Ess-toh noh ess loh keh eh orr-deh-na-doh)*

It's tough, cold, off
Está duro, frío, podrido *(Ess-ta doo-roh, free-yoh, pod-ree-doh)*

What do you recommend?
¿Qué me recomienda? *(Keh meh rekko-m'yen-da)*

Can I have the bill please?
¿Me trae la cuenta, por favor? *(Meh tra-eh la kwen-ta, por fa-vor)*

We'd like to pay separately
Queremos pagar en forma separada *(Keh-reh-moss pa-garr en for-ma seppa-ra-da)*

There is a mistake
Hay un error *(Aee oon error)*

Thank you, that's for you
Gracias, esto es para usted *(Graas-yass, ess-toh ess parra oos-ted)*

Keep the change
Quédese con el cambio *(Keh-deh-seh kon ell kam-b'yoh)*

DRINKS
BEBIDAS

---

a beer/lager – large, small
una cerveza – grande, pequeña *(oona serr-veh-sa – grann-deh, peh-kehn-ya)*

glass (¼ litre) of cider
un vaso (un cuarto) de
sidra (oon _bah_-soh [oon
kwarr-toh] deh _seed_-ra)

a dry white wine
un vino blanco seco
(oon _bee_-noh _blang_-koh
sek-koh)

a sweet white wine
un vino blanco dulce
(oon _bee_-noh _blang_-koh
dool-seh)

a light red wine
un vino tinto ligero
(oon _bee_-noh _teen_-toh
lee-_kheh_-roh)

a full-bodied red wine
un vino tinto con cuerpo
(oon _bee_-noh _teen_-toh
kon _kwerr_-poh)

new wine
vino nuevo (_bee_-noh
nweh-voh)

house wine
vino de la casa (_bee_-noh
della _ka_-sa)

**a glass of wine with
soda water**
un vaso de vino con soda
(oon _ba_-soh deh
bee-noh kon _soh_-da)

punch
ponche (_ponn_-cheh)

champagne
espumante
(es-poo-_man_-teh)

a brandy
un brandy (oon brandy)

a whisky with ice
un whisky con hielo (oon
whisky kon _yeh_-loh)

liqueur
licor (lee-_korr_)

a glass
una copa (oona _kop_-pa)

a bottle
una botella
(oona boh-_tey_-ya)

**a mineral water –
still, sparkling**
agua mineral – sin gas,
con gas
(_agwa mee-neh-_rall_ –
seen gass, _kon_ gass)

tap water
agua del grifo
(_agwa dell _gree_-foh)

fruit juice
zumo de fruta
(_soo_-moh deh _froo_-ta)

cola and lemonade
cola y limonada (*koh-la ee lee-moh-na-da*)

another ... please
otro ... por favor (*otroh ... por fa-vor*)

too cold
demasiado frío (*deh-mass-ya-doh free-yoh*)

not cold enough
no está suficientemente frío (*noh ess-ta soo-fee-s'yen-teh-menteh free-yoh*)

> ## FOOD
> COMIDA

Soup, Cream Soup
Sopa, Sopa Crema
(*soh-pa, soh-pa kreh-ma*)

potato soup, mushroom soup
sopa de patata/papa, sopa de champiñones (*soh-pa deh pa-ta-ta/pappa, soh-pa deh cham-peen-yoh-ness*)

cabbage soup
sopa de repollo (*soh-pa deh reh-poy-yoh*

pea, bean, lentil soup
sopa de guisantes, frijoles, lentejas (*soh-pa deh gee-san-tess, free-kho-less, len-teh-khass*)

consommé
consomé (*kon-som-meh*)

Fish
Pescado (*pess-ka-doh*)

bass
corvina (*korr-vee-na*)

sea bass
dorado (*doh-ra-doh*)

cod
bacalao (*ba-ka-laoo*)

snapper
pargo (*parr-goh*)

salmon
salmón (*sal-mon*)

swordfish
pez espada (*pess ess-pa-da*)

trout
trucha (*troo-cha*)

catfish
bagre (*baa-greh*)

tuna
atún (a-_toon_)

fried, grilled, sautéed
frito, a la parrilla, salteado
(_free_-toh, alla pa-_reey_-ya,
sal-teh-_ya_-doh)

POULTRY
AVES (_a_-vess)

chicken
pollo (_poy_-yoh)

**crumbed roasted
chicken**
pollo asado empanizado
(_poy_-yoh a-_sa_-doh
em-pa-nee-_sa_-doh)

duck
pato (_pa_-toh)

goose
ganso (_gann_-soh)

roasted
asado (a-_sa_-doh)

MEAT
CARNE (_karr_-neh)

veal
carne de ternera
(_karr_-neh deh terr-_neh_-ra)

sausage
salchicha (sal-_chee_-cha)

veal sausage
salchicha de ternera
(sal-_chee_-cha deh
terr-_neh_-ra)

mutton, lamb
carne de cordero (_karr_-
neh deh kor-_deh_-roh)

beef
carne de vaca (_karr_-neh
deh _ba_-ka)

pork
carne de cerdo (_karr_-neh
deh _serr_-doh)

venison
venado (be-_na_-doh)

steak
bistek (bee-_steck_)

meat balls/cakes
bolas de carne
(_boh_-las deh _karr_-neh)

**well done, medium,
rare**
bien hecho, medio
hecho, poco hecho
(b'_yen_ _etch_oh, _med_-yo
_etch_oh, _poh_-koh _etch_oh)

boiled, stewed
hervido, guisado (err-_vee_-
doh, gee-_sa_-doh)

smoked meats
carnes ahumadas(*karr-ness aoo-ma-dass*)

platter of cold meats
un plato de carnes frías
(*oon pla-toh deh karr-ness free-yass*)

PASTA AND RICE
PASTA Y ARROZ
(*pas-ta ee ar-ross*)

pasta made with cottage cheese
pasta hecha con queso untable (*pas-ta etcha kon keh-soh oon-ta-bleh*)

pasta with tomato sauce
pasta con salsa de tomate (*pas-ta kon sal-sa deh toh-ma-teh*)

rice
arroz (*ar-ross*)

VEGETABLES, SALAD AND FRUIT
VERDURAS, ENSALADA Y FRUTA (*ber-doo-rass, en-sa-la-da ee froo-ta*)

eggplant
berenjena
(*beh-ren-khe-na*)

onion
cebolla (*seh-boy-ya*)

cabbage
repollo (*reh-poy-yoh*)

cauliflower
coliflor (*kollee-florr*)

carrots
zanahorias
(*sana-oh-r'yas*)

green beans
frijoles verdes (*free-kho-less berr-dess*)

leeks
puerros (*pwer-ross*)

asparagus
espárragos
(*es-parra-goss*)

peppers
pimienta (*peem-yen-ta*)

pumpkin
zapallo, calabaza
(*sa-pay-yoh, kalla-ba-sa*)

potatoes – boiled, fried, mashed
patatas/papas – hervidas, fritas, puré de papas
(*pa-ta-tass/pappass – err-vee-dass, free-tass, poo-reh deh pappass*)

lettuce
lechuga (leh-_choo_-ga)

beetroot
remolacha (remmo-_la_-cha)

cucumber
pepino (peh-_pee_-noh)

root celery
apio (_ap_-yoh)

lemon
limón (lee-_mon_)

grapefruit
toronja (toh-_ronn_-khah)

apples
manzanas (man-_sa_-nass)

pears
peras (_peh_-rass)

bananas
bananos ba-_na_-noss)

pineapple
piñas/ananás
(_peen_-yass, a-na-_nass_)

cherries
cerezas (seh-_reh_-sass)

strawberries
fresas, frutillas
(_freh_-sass, froo-_tee_-yass)

apricots
albaricoques/damascos
(al-barree-_koh_-kess,
da-_mass_-koss)

peaches
melocotones/duraznos
(melloh-koh-_toh_-ness/
doo-_ras_-noss)

raspberries
frambuesas
(fram-_bweh_-sass)

blackberries
moras (_moh_-rass)

plums
ciruelas (seer-_weh_-lass)

prunes
ciruelas pasas
(seer-_weh_-lass _pas_sas)

grapes
uvas (_oo_-vass)

dried fruit
fruta seca/disecada
(_froo_-ta _seh_-ka/
dee-seh-_ka_-da)

**passion fruit,
grenadilla**
maracuyá (ma-ra-coo-_ya_)

cranberries
arándanos (a-_ran_-da-noss)

COMER Y BEBER

DESSERTS AND CAKES
POSTRES Y PASTELES

fruit salad
ensalada de frutas *(en-sa-la-da deh froo-tass)*

jelly
gelatina *(khe-la-tee-na)*

crème caramel
flan *(flan)*

meringue
merengue *(meh-reng-geh)*

pastry with apples and raisins
tarta de manzanas *(tarr-ta deh man-sa-nass)*

light fruitcake
tarta de frutas *(tarr-ta deh froo-tass)*

plain sponge with crumble topping
bizcocho *(bees-kotchoh)*

fruit flan
flan de frutas *(flan deh froo-tass)*

marble cake
torta marmolada *(torr-ta marr-moh-la-da)*

cheesecake
pastel de queso *(pass-tell deh keh-soh)*

gateau with cherries and cream
torta con cerezas y crema *(torr-ta con seh-reh-sass ee kreh-ma)*

poppyseed cake
torta con semillas de amapola *(torr-ta con seh-mee-yass deh amma-poh-la)*

honey and almond tart
tarta de miel y almendras *(tarr-ta deh myell ee al-men-drass)*

sponge cake with chocolate
bizcocho con chocolate *(bees-kotcho con chokkoh-la-teh)*

flan with raspberry jam
flan con jalea de frambuesa *(flan con kha-leh-ya deh fram-bweh-sa)*

gingerbread biscuits
galletitas de jengibre *(ga-yeh-tee-tass deh khen-khee-breh)*

MONEY
DINERO

bureau de change
cambio/casa de
cambio (_kam-b'yoh/_
ka-sa deh kam-b'yoh)

cash dispenser/ATM
cajero automático
(_ka-kheh-roh aoo-toh-_
ma-tee-koh)

Where can I change money?
¿Dónde puedo cambiar
dinero? (_Donn-deh_
pweh-doh kam-b'yarr
dee-neh-roh)

Where is an ATM, a bank?
¿Dónde hay un cajero
automático, un banco?
(_Donn-deh aee_
oon ka-kheh-roh
aoo-toh-ma-tee-koh,
oon bang-koh)

When does the bank open/close?
¿A qué hora abre/cierra
el banco? (_A keh oh-ra_
a-breh/s'yer-ra ell
bang-koh)

How much commission do you charge?
¿Cuánta comisión
cobran? (_Kwan-ta_
ko-mee-s'yon kob-ran)

I want to ...
Quiero ... (_Kyeh-roh ..._)

◆ **cash a traveller's cheque**
◆ cambiar cheques de
viajero (_kam-b'yarr_
cheh-kess deh
bee-a-kheh-roh)

◆ **change $50**
◆ cambiar cincuenta
dólares (_kam-b'yarr_
seeng-kwen-ta
dolla-ress)

◆ **make a transfer**
◆ hacer una transferencia
(_a-serr oona trans-_
feh-ren-s'ya)

POST OFFICE
OFICINA DE CORREOS

How much is ...?
¿Cuánto cuesta ...?
(_Kwan-toh kwess-ta_)

◆ **a letter**
◆ una carta (_oona karr-ta_)

MONEY AND SHOPPING

- **a postcard to ...**
- una postal a ...
  (oona poss-*tal* a ...)

- **a small parcel**
- un paquete pequeño
  (oon pa-*keh*-teh peh-*kehn*-yoh)

Where can I buy stamps?
¿Dónde puedo comprar sellos? (*Donn*-deh pweh-doh kom-*prarr* *sey*-yoss)

SHOPPING
COMPRAS

What does it cost?
¿Cuánto cuesta? (*Kwan*-toh *kwess*-ta)

How much is it (total)?
¿Cuánto es todo? (*Kwan*-toh ess *toddoh*)

I need a receipt
Necesito un recibo (ne-seh-*see*-toh oon reh-*see*-boh)

Do you accept credit cards?
¿Se aceptan tarjetas de crédito? (Seh a-*sep*-tan tarr-*kheh*-tass deh *kreh*-dee-toh)

Do you take traveller's cheques?
¿Se aceptan cheques de viajero? (Seh a-*sep*-tan *cheh*-kess deh bee-a-*kheh*-roh)

Does that include VAT?
¿El impuesto de venta está incluido? (Ell eem-*pwess*-toh de *ben*-ta ess-*ta* een-kloo-*ee*-doh)

Do you need a deposit?
¿Necesita un depósito? (ne-seh-*see*-ta oon deh-*poh*-see-toh)

Can you wrap it up for me?
¿Puedes envolverlo? (*Pweh*-dess em-bol-*verr*-loh)

This isn't what I want
Esto no es lo que yo quiero (*Ess*-toh *noh* ess loh keh yoh k'*yeh*-roh)

This isn't correct (bill)
Esto no es correcto (la cuenta) (*Ess*-toh *noh* ess koh-*rek*-toh)

I want my money back
Quiero de vuelta mi dinero *(K'yeh-roh deh bwell-ta mee dee-neh-roh)*

This is ...
Esto está ... *(Ess-toh ess-ta ...)*

◆ **broken**
◆ roto *(roh-toh)*

◆ **damaged**
◆ dañado *(dan-ya-doh*

Can you repair it?
¿Puede repararlo? *(Pweh-deh reppa-rarr-loh)*

BUYING FOOD
COMPRA DE COMIDA

Where can I buy ...?
¿Dónde puedo comprar ...? *(Donn-deh pweh-doh kom-prarr)*

◆ **bread**
◆ pan *(pan)*

◆ **cake**
◆ pastel/torta *(pass-tell/torr-ta)*

◆ **cheese**
◆ queso *(keh-soh)*

◆ **butter**
◆ mantequilla *(man-teh-kee-ya)*

◆ **milk**
◆ leche *(letcheh)*

◆ **water**
◆ agua *(agwa)*

◆ **wine**
◆ vino *(bee-noh)*

◆ **sparkling wine**
◆ vino espumante *(bee-noh es-poo-man-teh)*

◆ **beer**
◆ cerveza *(serr-veh-sa)*

◆ **fruit juice**
◆ jugo/zumo de fruta *(khoo-goh/soo-moh deh froo-ta)*

◆ **meat**
◆ carne *(karr-neh)*

◆ **ham**
◆ jamón *(kha-monn)*

◆ **polony/cold meats**
◆ carnes frías *(karr-ness free-yass)*

◆ **vegetables**
◆ verduras *(ber-doo-rass)*

- **fruit**
- fruta (*froo*-ta)

- **eggs**
- huevos (oo*weh*-voss)

I'll take ...
Llevo ... (*Yeh*-voh ...)

- **one kilo**
- un kilo (oon *kee*-loh)

- **three slices**
- tres rebanadas (*tress* rebba-*na*-dass)

- **a portion of**
- una porción de (oona por-s'*yon* deh)

- **a packet of**
- un paquete de (oon pa-*keh*-teh deh)

- **a dozen**
- una docena (oona doh-*seh*-na)

BUYING CLOTHES
COMPRA DE ROPA

Can I try this on?
¿Puedo probarlo? (*Pweh*-doh proh-*barr*-loh)

It is ...
Es ... (*Ess* ...)

- **too big**
- demasiado grande (deh-mass-*ya*-doh *grann*-deh)

- **too small**
- demasiado pequeño (deh-mass-*ya*-doh peh-*kehn*-yoh)

- **too tight**
- demasiado ajustado (deh-mass-*ya*-doh a-khoos-*ta*-doh)

- **too wide**
- demasiado ancho (deh-mass-*ya*-doh *an*choh)

- **too expensive**
- demasiado caro (deh-mass-*ya*-doh *ka*-roh)

I'll take ...
Llevo ... (*Yeh*-voh ...)

- **this one**
- éste/ésta (*ess*-teh/*ess*-ta

- **size 40**
- talla 40 (*tay*-ya kwa-*ren*-ta)

- **two**
- dos (*doss*)

CLOTHING SIZES – TALLAS DE ROPA

Women's Wear

UK	Cont. Europe	USA
10	38	8
12	40	10
14	42	12
16	44	14
18	46	16

Menswear

UK	Cont. Europe	USA
36	46	36
38	48	38
40	50	40
42	52	42
44	54	44
46	56	46

Men's Shirts

UK	Cont. Europe	USA
14	36	14
14.5	37	14.5
15	38	15
15.5	39	15.5
16	41	16
17	43	17

Shoes

UK	Cont. Europe	USA
5	39	6
6	40	7
7	41	8
8	42	9
9	43	10
10	44	11
11	45	12

SIGHTSEEING
TURISMO

tourist office
oficina de turismo *(offee-see-na deh too-rees-moh)*

Do you have brochures/leaflets?
¿Tiene folletos? *(T'yen-neh foy-yeh-toss)*

I/We want to visit ...
Queremos visitar ... *(Kehr-reh-moss bee-see-tarr ...)*

When is it open/closed?
¿A qué hora abre/cierra? *(A keh oh-ra ab-reh/s'yer-ra)*

What does it cost?
¿Cuánto cuesta? *(Kwan-toh kwess-ta)*

Are there any reductions for ...?
¿Hay descuento para ...? *(Aee des-kwen-toh parra)*

♦ **children**
♦ niños *(neen-yoss)*

♦ **senior citizens**
♦ jubilados *(khoo-bee-la-doss)*

♦ **students**
♦ estudiantes *(es-toodee-yan-tess)*

Are there any tours?
¿Hay visitas guiadas? *(Aee bee-see-tass gee-ya-dass)*

When does the bus depart/return?
¿Cuándo sale/regresa el autobús? *(Kwan-doh sa-leh/reh-gres-sa ell aoo-toh-booss)*

From where does the bus leave?
¿De dónde sale el autobús? *(Deh donn-deh sa-leh ell aoo-toh-booss)*

Where is the museum?
¿Dónde está el museo? *(Donn-deh ess-ta ell moo-seh-yoh)*

How much is the entrance fee?
¿Cuánto cuesta la entrada? *(Kwan-toh kwess-ta la en-tra-da)*

ENTERTAINMENT
DIVERSIÓN

Is there a list of cultural events?
¿Hay una lista/guía de eventos culturales?
(_Aee_ oona _lees_-ta/_gee_-ya deh eh-_ven_-toss kool-too-_ra_-less)

Are there any festivals?
¿Hay algún festival?
(_Aee_ al-_goon_ fes-tee-_val_)

I'd like to go to ...
Quiero ir ... (K'_yeh_-roh eer ...)

◆ **the theatre**
◆ al teatro (al teh-_a_-tro)

◆ **the opera**
◆ a la ópera
(alla _oh_-peh-ra)

◆ **the ballet**
◆ al ballet (al ba-_yeh_)

◆ **the cinema/movies**
◆ al cine (al _see_-neh)

◆ **a concert**
◆ a un concierto
(a oon kon-s'_yer_-toh)

Do I have to book?
¿Debo reservar?
(_Debboh_ reh-ser-_varr_)

How much are the tickets?
¿Cuánto cuestan los tiquetes?
(_Kwan_-toh _kwess_-tan loss tee-_ket_-tess)

Two tickets for ...
Dos tiquetes para ...
(_Doss_ tee-_ket_-tess parra)

◆ **tonight**
◆ esta noche (_ess_-ta _not_cheh)

◆ **tomorrow night**
◆ mañana por la noche
(man-_ya_-na porr la _not_cheh)

◆ **the early show**
◆ la matiné (la ma-tee-_neh_)

◆ **the late show**
◆ el espectáculo más tarde (ell es-pek-_ta_-coo-loh _mahss_ tarr-deh)

When does the performance start/end?
¿A qué hora comienza/termina la función? (A keh _oh_-ra koh-m'_yen_-sa/_terr_-mee-na la foon-s'_yon_)

Where is ...?
¿Dónde hay ...?
(*Donn*-deh *aee* ...)

- **a good bar**
- un buen bar (*oon bwen barr*)

- **good live music**
- buena música en vivo (*bweh*-na *moo*-see-ka en *bee*-voh)

Is it ...?
Es/Está ...? (*Ess*/Ess-*ta* ...)

- **expensive**
- caro (*ka*-roh)

- **noisy, crowded**
- ruidoso, muy lleno (*rooee-doh*-soh, *mooee yen*-noh)

How do I get there?
¿Cómo llego allí? (*kom*-moh *yeh*-goh a-*yee*)

SPORT
DEPORTES

Where can we ...?
¿Dónde podemos ...?
(*Donn*-deh poh-*deh*-moss)

- **go diving**
- bucear (*boo-seyarr*)

- **play tennis/golf**
- jugar al tenis/golf (*khoo-garr* al *ten*-nees/golf)

- **go swimming**
- nadar (*na-darr*)

- **go fishing**
- pescar (*pess-karr*)

- **go riding**
- cabalgar (*ka-bal-garr*)

- **go cycling**
- andar/montar en bicicleta (*an-darr*/mon-*tarr* en bee-see-*kleh*-ta)

- **hire bicycles**
- alquilar bicicletas (*al-kee-larr* bee-see-*kleh*-tass)

- **hire tackle**
- alquilar equipos de pesca (*al-kee-larr* eh-*kee*-poss deh *pess*-ka)

- **hire golf clubs**
- alquilar palos de golf (*al-kee-larr* pa-loss deh *golf*)

- **hire a surfboard**
- alquilar una tabla de surf (*al-kee-larr* oona *tab*-la de soorf)

- **hire a boat**
- alquilar un barco/un bote/una lancha *(al-kee-larr oon barr-koh/oon boh-teh/oona lan-cha)*

- **hire skates**
- alquilar patines *(al-kee-larr pa-tee-ness)*

- **hire an umbrella**
- alquilar un parasol/sombrilla *(al-kee-larr oon parra-sol/som-bree-ya)*

- **hire a deck chair**
- alquilar una silla para el sol *(al-kee-larr oona see-ya parra ell sol)*

How much is it ...?
¿Cuánto cuesta ...? *(Kwan-toh kwess-ta ...)*

- **per hour**
- por hora *(porr oh-ra)*

- **per day**
- por día *(porr dee-ya)*

- **per session/game**
- por sesión/juego *(porr sess-yon/khweh-goh)*

Is it ...?
Es ...? *(Ess ...)*

- **deep**
- profundo *(proh-foon-doh)*

- **clean**
- limpio *(leem-pyoh)*

- **cold**
- frío *(free-yoh)*

How do we get there?
¿Cómo llegamos allí? *(Koh-moh yeh-ga-moss a-yee)*

No swimming/diving
Prohibido nadar/zambullirse *(Pro-ee-bee-doh na-darr/sam-boo-yeer-seh)*

Are there currents?
¿Hay corrientes? *(Aee korr-yen-tess)*

Do I need a fishing permit?
¿Necesito un permiso de pesca? *(Ne-seh-see-toh oon per-mee-soh deh pess-ka)*

Where can I get one?
¿Dónde puedo obtenerlo? *(Donn-deh pweh-doh ob-teh-nerr-lo)*

68

Is there a guide for walks?
¿Hay un guía para las caminatas? *(Aee oon gee-ya parra lass kamee-na-tass)*

Do I need walking boots?
¿Necesito botas para senderismo? *(neh-seh-see-toh boh-tass parra sen-deh-rees-moh)*

How much is it to hire a court?
¿Cuánto cuesta alquilar una cancha? *(Kwan-toh kwess-ta al-kee-larr oona kann-cha)*

Can I hire some balls?
¿Puedo alquilar unas pelotas? *(Pweh-doh al-kee-larr oonas peh-loh-tass)*

hard court
cancha dura *(kann-cha doo-ra)*

to play doubles
jugar dobles *(khoo-garr dob-less)*

I'm a beginner
Soy principiante *(Soy preen-see-p'yan-teh)*

What's the score?
¿Cuál es el marcador? *(Kwal ess ell mar-ka-dorr)*

It was a draw
Fue un empate *(Fweh oon em-pa-teh)*

I follow ...
Soy aficionado/a ... *(Soy a-fee-s'yon-na-doh/da ...)*

We want to go ...
Queremos ir ... *(Keh-reh-moss eer ...)*

- ◆ **hiking**
- ◆ de senderismo/de caminata *(deh sen-deh-rees-moh/ deh kamee-na-ta)*

- ◆ **sailing**
- ◆ a navegar *(a na-veh-garr)*

- ◆ **skating**
- ◆ a patinar *(a pa-tee-narr)*

- ◆ **water-skiing**
- ◆ a hacer esquí acuático *(a a-serr es-kee akoo-a-tee-koh)*

PHARMACY/ CHEMIST
FARMACIA

health shop
tienda de medicinas
naturales *(t'yen-da deh
meddee-see-nass
na-too-ra-less)*

**Have you got
something for ...?**
¿Tiene algo para ...?
(T'yn-neh al-goh parra ...)

◆ **diarrhoea**
◆ diarrea *(dee-ya-reh-ya)*

◆ **cold, flu**
◆ resfriado, gripe *(ress-
free-a-doh, gree-peh)*

◆ **headache**
◆ dolor de cabeza
(doh-lorr de ka-beh-sa)

◆ **a sore throat**
◆ dolor de garganta
*(doh-lorr de
garr-gan-ta)*

◆ **stomachache**
◆ dolor de estómago
*(doh-lorr de
es-toh-ma-goh)*

◆ **car sickness**
◆ mareo de viaje en
coche *(ma-reh-yoh
deh bee-a-kheh en
kotcheh)*

I need ...
Necesito ...
(Ne-seh-see-toh ...)

◆ **indigestion tablets**
◆ tabletas para
indigestión
*(tab-leh-tass parra
een-dee-khess-t'yon)*

◆ **laxative**
◆ laxante *(lax-an-teh)*

◆ **sleeping tablets**
◆ tabletas para dormir
*(tab-leh-tass parra
dorr-meer)*

◆ **a painkiller**
◆ un analgésico *(oon
annal-kheh-see-koh)*

**Is it safe for
children?**
¿Es seguro para niños?
*(Ess seh-goo-roh parra
neen-yoss)*

I'm a diabetic
Soy diabético *(Soy
dee-ya-bet-tee-koh)*

I have high blood pressure
Sufro de presión alta
(Soo-froh deh pres-see-on alta)

I'm allergic to ...
Soy alérgico a ... *(Soy a-lerr-khee-koh a ...)*

DOCTOR
MÉDICO

I am ill
Estoy enfermo
(Estoy en-ferr-moh)

I need a doctor
Necesito un médico
(Ne-seh-see-toh oon med-dee-koh)

He/she has a high temperature
Tiene fiebre
(T'yen-neh fee-eb-reh)

It hurts
Duele *(Dweh-leh)*

I am going to be sick!
¡Voy a vomitar!
(Boy a bo-mee-tarr)

dentist
dentista *(den-tees-ta)*

I have toothache
Me duelen los dientes
(Meh dweh-len loss dee-en-tess)

optometrist
optometrista
(op-toh-meh-trees-ta)

HOSPITAL
HOSPITAL

Will I have to go to hospital?
¿Debo ir al hospital? *(Deb-boh eer al oss-pee-tal)*

Where is the hospital?
¿Dónde está el hospital?
(Donn-deh ess-ta ell oss-pee-tal)

Which ward?
¿Cuál sala? *(Kwal sa-la)*

When are visiting hours?
¿Cuál es el horario de visita? *(Kwal ess ell oh-raar-yoh deh bee-see-ta)*

Where is casualty?
¿Dónde están las emergencias?
(Donn-deh ess-tan lass em-mer-khens-yass)

POLICE
POLICÍA

Call the police
Llame a la policía (*Ya*-meh
alla pollee-*see*-ya)

I have been robbed
Me han robado
(*Meh* an ro-*ba*-doh)

My car has been stolen
Han robado mi coche (*An*
ro-*ba*-doh mee *kot*cheh)

My car has been broken into
Han robado de mi coche
(*An* ro-*ba*-doh deh mee
*kot*cheh)

I want to report a theft
Quiero denunciar un robo
(*K'yeh*-roh deh-noon-
see-*yarr* oon *roh*-boh)

I have been attacked
Me han atacado
(*Meh* an atta-*ka*-doh)

I have been raped
Me han violado
(*Meh* an bee-oh-la-*doh*)

Where is the police station?
¿Dónde está la oficina de
policía/comisaría? (*Donn*-
deh ess-*ta* la offee-*see*-
na deh pollee-*see*-ya)

EMERGENCIES
EMERGENCIAS

Call an ambulance
Llame una ambulancia
(*Ya*-meh oona
amboo-*lan*-s'ya)

There's been an accident
Hubo un accidente
(*Oo*-boh oon
ak-see-*den*-teh)

Someone is injured
Alguien está herido
(*Al*-gee-yen ess-*ta*
eh-*ree*-doh)

Hurry up!
¡Date prisa!
(*Da*-teh *pree*-sa)

Could you please help me?
¿Puede ayudarme por
favor? (*Pweh*-deh a-yoo-
darr-meh por fa-*vor*)

Help!
¡Ayúdeme!
(a-yoo-deh-meh)

This is an emergency!
¡Hay una emergencia!
*(Aee oona
em-merr-khen-s'ya)*

My son/daughter is missing
Mi hijo/hija está desaparecido/a
*(Mee ee-khoh/ee-kha
ess-ta dessa-parreh-
see-doh/da)*

I need a report for my insurance
Necesito un informe para mi seguro *(Ne-seh-see-
toh oon een-forr-meh
parra mee seh-goo-roh)*

I want to phone my embassy
Quiero llamar a mi embajada *(K'yeh-roh ya-
marr mee em-ba-kha-da)*

I am lost
Estoy perdido
(Estoy per-dee-doh)

He/she is ill
Está enfermo/a
(Ess-ta en-ferr-moh/ma)

FIRE DEPARTMENT
BOMBEROS

Fire!
¡Fuego! *(Fweh-goh)*

Look out!
¡Cuídese! *(Kee-deh-seh)*

Call the fire department
Llame a los bomberos
*(Ya-meh a loss
bom-beh-ross)*

It's an electrical fire
Es un incendio eléctrico
*(Ess oon een-senn-d'yoh
elek-tree-koh)*

The address is ...
La dirección es ... *(La
dee-rek-s'yon ess ...)*

I need ...
Necesito ...
(Ne-seh-see-toh ...)

♦ **a fire extinguisher**
♦ un extintor
(oon ex-teen-torr)

♦ **medical assistance**
♦ ayuda médica
(a-yoo-da meh-dee-ka)

74

THE HUMAN BODY
EL CUERPO HUMANO

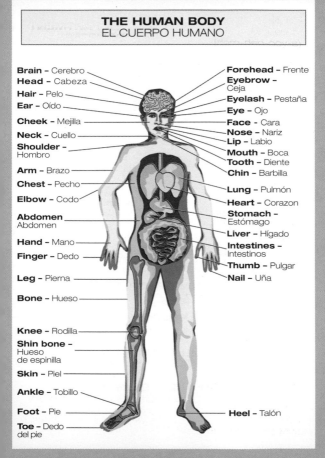

Brain – Cerebro
Head – Cabeza
Hair – Pelo
Ear – Oído
Cheek – Mejilla
Neck – Cuello
Shoulder – Hombro
Arm – Brazo
Chest – Pecho
Elbow – Codo
Abdomen Abdomen
Hand – Mano
Finger – Dedo
Leg – Pierna
Bone – Hueso
Knee – Rodilla
Shin bone – Hueso de espinilla
Skin – Piel
Ankle – Tobillo
Foot – Pie
Toe – Dedo del pie

Forehead – Frente
Eyebrow – Ceja
Eyelash – Pestaña
Eye – Ojo
Face – Cara
Nose – Nariz
Lip – Labio
Mouth – Boca
Tooth – Diente
Chin – Barbilla
Lung – Pulmón
Heart – Corazon
Stomach – Estómago
Liver – Hígado
Intestines – Intestinos
Thumb – Pulgar
Nail – Uña
Heel – Talón

75

FORMS OF ADDRESS
TRATOS

There are two ways of translating the English word 'you'. The formal way is *Usted* (which is abbreviated *Ud.*). This form of address is a sign of courtesy and respect, and would normally be used when addressing elderly people, teachers, bosses, shopkeepers and people you don't know very well, especially if they are older than you.

The less formal translation of 'you' is *tú*, which is the form generally used when addressing family, friends and people you know well. Nowadays *tú* is used much more often than before.

GREETING PEOPLE
SALUDOS

When it comes to greeting each other, the Hispanic people are rather formal, and the usual form of greeting is to shake hands. This applies to both young and old people.

Hugging is also a very Hispanic custom, and men who know each other well will usually hug each other.

Kissing varies from country to country. In Spain a greeting will usually consist of two kisses, one on each cheek, whereas in most Latin American countries there will only be one kiss on the cheek.

Eye contact is important, and Latinos expect you to make eye contact whenever you speak to them. In many societies it is in fact considered rude not to establish and maintain eye contact.

MANNERS
ETIQUETA

The well-known fiery Latin temperament means that Spanish people are usually quite outspoken and direct. This same temperament also leads to rather high levels of noise. The people speak loudly, and the drivers generally hoot a lot, so don't expect an especially quiet time when visiting a Spanish-speaking country!

On the other hand, there is the very Spanish custom of the *siesta*, and in most Spanish-speaking countries everything comes to a standstill during the hottest part of the day, when people have a rest.

Spanish-speaking people can be very helpful towards strangers. The more you try to talk to them, no matter how excruciating your Spanish pronunciation is, the more they will want to help you. They may even offer to acompany you to whichever place it is you are trying to find. So it would be well worth your while to learn the basics of the language before you embark on a visit to a Spanish-speaking country, whether you are going on holiday or on a business trip. If you make the effort it will be appreciated.

COMMUNICATION
COMUNICACIÓN

There are many Spanish words that cannot be simply and literally translated into English, for example words such as *relación* (relation-ship), *comida* (food) or *paseo* (a walk), which have many more connotations attached to them than their literal meanings tell us.

The Spanish phrase *dar un paseo*, for instance, literally means 'to go for a walk', but it carries with it a wealth of social images such as people out for a leisurely walk with their family and friends, sitting and relaxing at

a sidewalk café, seeing people and in turn
being seen by others. In Spanish-speaking
countries to go for a walk means something
entirely different to what it means to English-
speaking people.

FOOD AND MEALS
COMIDAS

Just as the geography of the Hispanic world
is very extensive, so too is its cuisine. If you
talk about Spanish food in the United States
of America, you are probably referring to
Mexican food. But the food in Mexico is very
different from the food in Spain. Many
Mexican dishes are based on the tortilla. The
Mexican tortilla is a pancake made of maize,
whereas the Spanish tortilla is an omelette
made of potatoes. In the same way there are
many differences between Mexican food and
Chilean food, as there are between Chilean
food and Argentinian food.

In Spain you will be able to sample a wide
variety of delicious *tapas*, or snacks. These
can range from a simple dish of olives to
more elegant offerings such as bits of spicy
sausage, meatballs in sauce, various

cheeses or beautifully prepared fish snacks. The name *tapas* literally means 'lids', as these snacks originated in the 19th century when bartenders used to place a small dish of nuts on top of a beer glass, probably to keep the flies out!

Spain is also famous for its *paella*, a wonderful dish based on rice with the addition of meat, seafood and vegetables. The name comes from the Spanish *para ella*, meaning 'for her'. The dish originated from the old custom of husbands taking over the cooking duties from their wives on a Sunday in order to give the lady of the house a well-earned break. The elegant *paella* you will encounter in restaurants nowadays probably bears little resemblance to the concoction from whence it came, because the original *paella* was made with whatever leftovers the man of the house could lay his hands on, whereas today it is made with fresh ingredients.

Meal times vary enormously from country to country and also from season to season. Dinner is usually quite late – in most cases well after 20:00 and often as late as 22:00 – especially in summer.

OFFICIAL HOLIDAYS
FIESTAS OFICIALES

New Year's Day
Día de año nuevo
(1 January)
Exuberant parties and dances are held on 31 December – *la noche de año viejo* – so most people spend New Year's Day recovering.

Juan Santamaría Day
Día de Juan Santamaría
(11 April)
Honoring a national hero who died in the Battle of Rivas in 1856.

Easter
Semana Santa
(March/April)
The Easter weekend includes Good Friday – *Viernes Santo* – which is preceded by *Jueves Santo* ('Good Thursday'), as well as Easter Sunday (*Domingo de Pascua*) and Easter Monday (*Lunes Santo*). Special Easter church services are held all over Spain.

May Day, Labour Day
Fiesta del Trabajo
(1 May)
An official holiday for the workers.

Guanacaste Day
(25 July)
This holiday commemorates the annexation of Guanacaste to Costa Rica.

Mother's Day
Día de la Madre
(15 August)
An official holiday.

Independence Day
Día de la Independencia
(15 September)
Nationwide celebrations. Independence from Spain in 1821.

Columbus Day
Día de las Culturas
(12 October)
In 1504 Christopher Columbus set foot in Limón.

Christmas
Navidad
(25 December)
From the first Sunday of Advent private and public festivities mark this special season, leading up to the highlight of Christmas Eve (*Nochebuena*).

NATIONAL DAYS
FIESTAS NACIONALES

Día Nacional en Costa Rica (Día de la Independencia)
(15 September)
Independence Day, the national day of Costa Rica.

Other national days:
27 February **Dominican Republic**
14 May **Paraguay**
25 May **Argentina**
5 July **Venezuela**
20 July **Colombia**
28 July **Peru**
6 August **Bolivia**
10 August **Ecuador**

25 August **Uruguay**

15 September **El Salvador, Guatemala, Honduras, Nicaragua**

16 September **Mexico**

18 September **Chile**

12 October **Spain, Equatorial Guinea**

SPECIAL FESTIVALS
FESTIVALES ESPECIALES

Fiestas de Palmares, Alajuela

(Second week in January)

Every year in the dry season, thousands of people arrive in the town of Palmares (west of San José). There are bullfights, horse parades (*tope*) and more.

Fiestas de Santa Cruz, Guanacaste

(Third week in January)

This is a religious festival and is held in honor of the Christ of Esquipulas. The celebrations include bullfights, horse parades (*tope*) and music.

Carnavales de Puntarenas

(Second week in February)

This carnival takes place in the Pacific Region, approximately 120km (75 miles) to the west of San José. The festivities usually take the form of concerts, lively dancing and colourful parades.

Fiestas de Liberia, Guanacaste

(Third week in February)
Celebrated with folk dances, concerts and much more.

Semana Universitaria, San José

(April)
Parades, dancing and concerts take place at the University of Costa Rica, San Pedro.

Festividad de la Virgen del Mar, Puntarenas

(Second week in July)
A large number of boats are decorated in preparation for this festival, a typical regatta in the Golfo de Nicoya.

Romería a la Basílica de Nuestra Señora de los Angeles, Cartago

(2 August)
This is a pilgrimage to commemorate a miraculous appearance in 1635 of the Virgin of Los Angeles. It is also known as the Feast of Patroness of Costa Rica 'La Negrita'. Thousands of worshippers walk from San José to Cartago each year to honour her.

Carnavales de Limón

(Third week in October)
This carnival takes place in Puerto Limón (in the Caribbean Region). There are dance contests and

various floats, and the carnival ends with a colourful parade.

Festival de la Luz, San José

(Second week in December)

During this festival, lights fill the avenues of San José. There are wonderful float parades, fireworks and a lot of lively music.

Carnavales de San José

(Last week in December)

This is the biggest carnival of all in Costa Rica. Dance troupes display their talents and the music is vibrant.

Tope Nacional

(Last week in December)

Horse parades (*tope*) and costumed riders take to the streets of San José.

Festejos Populares de San José

(Last week in December)

Festejos Populares are probably the best known and most popular celebrations in Costa Rica. The largest of these are held in Zapote, a suburb east of San José. These festivals also include concerts, dancing, fireworks and bullfights that run all day and well into the night.

ENGLISH → SPANISH

A

abbey abadía f
abortion aborto m
about (approximately) aproximadamente
above sobre
abroad en el extranjero
abscess absceso m
absolutely por supuesto, claro
accelerator acelerador m
accent acento m
accept aceptar
accident accidente m
accommodation alojamiento m
account cuenta f
accurate exacto
ache dolor m
adapter adaptador m
adhesive tape cinta adhesiva f
admission fee entrada f
adult (adj, n) adulto/a m/f
advance, in advance por adelantado
advertisement aviso m
advice consejo m
advise aconsejar
aeroplane avión m
afraid, be afraid of tener miedo
after después
afternoon tarde

afterwards después, luego
again otra vez
against contra
age edad f
agree estar de acuerdo
agreement acuerdo m
air aire m
air conditioning aire acondicionado
air ticket billete aéreo
airmail correo aéreo
airport aeropuerto m
aisle pasillo m
aisle seat asiento en el pasillo
all right vale, está bien
allow permitir, dejar
almond almendra f
almost casi
alone solo
already ya
also también
although a pesar de
altogether todo junto
always siempre
a.m. (before noon) por la mañana
am, I am yo soy/estoy
amazing fabuloso, maravilloso
amber ámbar m
ambulance ambulancia f
among dentro
amount monto m, cantidad f
anaesthetic anestético m

ancient viejo/a
and y
angry enfadado, enojado
animal animal m
ankle tobillo m
anniversary
  aniversario m
annoy molestar
annual anual
another otro/a
answer (n) respuesta f
answer (vb) responder
ant hormiga
antacid antiácido
anybody cualquiera
anything cualquier cosa
apartment piso m,
  apartemento m
apology disculpa f
appendicitis apendicitis f
appointment cita f
approximately
  aproximadamente
apron delantal m
are son, están
area barrio m, área f
armchair sillón m
arrange arreglar
arrest arrestar
arrival llegada f
arrive llegar
art arte m
artist artista m/f
ask preguntar
astonishing fascinante
at en
attack (n) ataque m
attack (vb) atacar

attic ático m
audience audiencia f
aunt tía f
auto-teller cajero
  automático
autumn otoño m
available disponible
avalanche avalancha f
avenue avenida f
average promedio
avoid evitar
awake despertar
away fuera
awful feo/a, malo/a,
  terrible

B
baby food comida
  para bebé
back espalda f
backache dolor de
  espalda
backpack mochila f
bacon tocino m
bad malo/a
bag bolsa f
baggage equipaje m
baggage reclaim
  recolección de equipajes
bait cebo m, carnada f
bakery panadería f
balcony balcón m
ballpoint pen
  bolígrafo m, lapicera
Baltic Sea Mar Báltico
bandage venda f,
  vendaje m

ENGLISH → SPANISH

ENGLISH → SPANISH

bar of chocolate
  barra de chocolate
barber's shop barbería f
bark (vb) ladrar
barn granero m
barrel barril m
basement sótano m
basket cesta, canasta f
bath bañera f
bathroom baño m,
  servicios mpl
bay bahía f
bay leaf hoja de laurel
be ser, estar
beach playa f
bean haba f, judía f,
  frijol m
beard barba f
beautiful bonito/a,
  precioso/a, lindo/a
beauty salon
  salón de belleza
because porque
because of por
bed cama f
bed & breakfast
  pensión f
bed linen ropa de cama
bedspread cobertor
bee abeja f
beef carne de vaca f
beer cerveza f
before antes
beginner principiante m/f
behind detrás
Belgian (adj, n)
  belga m/f
Belgium Bélgica

believe creer
bell campana f
below bajo
belt cinturón m
bend doblar
beside junto a
bet apostar
better mejor
beyond más allá
bicycle bicicleta f
big gran, grande
bill cuenta f
bin cubo de la basura
binoculars binoculares,
  prismáticos mpl
bird pájaro m, ave f
birth nacimiento m
birth certificate
  certificado de nacimiento
birthday cumpleaños m
birthday card tarjeta
  de cumpleaños
birthday present
  regalo de cumpleaños
biscuit galleta f
bit un poco
bite (vb) morder
black negro/a
blackcurrant
  grosella negra
blanket manta f
bleach (vb) blanquear
bleed sangrar
blind (n) persiana
blind (adj) ciego/a
blister ampolla f
block of flats edificio
  de apartamentos

blocked cerrado/a, bloqueado
blood sangre f
blood pressure presión arterial
blouse blusa f
blow-dry secar
blue azul
blunt contundente
blusher colorete m
boar jabalí m
boarding card tarjeta de embarque
boarding house pensión f
boat barco m, bote m
boat trip viaje en barco
body cuerpo m
boil (n) furúnculo m
boil (vb) hervir
bone hueso m
bonnet (car) capó/capota m/f
book libro m
bookshop librería f
boots botas fpl
border borde m
boring aburrido, pesado/a
born nacer
borrow tomar prestado
both los dos, ambos
bottle botella f
bottle opener abridor de botellas
bottom (at the) al fondo
bow tie humita, pajarita f

bowl cuenco m
box caja f
boy niño m
boyfriend novio m
bra sostén m
bracelet pulsera f
brake (n) freno m
brake fluid líquido de freno
brake light luz de freno
branch (office) sucursal f
brand marca f
brandy brandy m
bread pan m
break romper
breakable se puede romper, frágil
breakdown (of car) avería f
breakdown van camion de reparación de averías
breakfast desayuno m
break-in robo m
breast pecho m, teta f
breathe respirar
breeze brisa f
brewery fábrica de cerveza
brick ladrillo m
bride novia f
bridegroom novio m
bridge puente m
briefcase maletín m
bright brillante
bring traer
bring in introducir

brochure folleto m
broken roto/a
bronchitis bronquitis f
brooch broche m
broom escoba f
brother hermano m
brother-in-law
  cuñado m
brown pardo/a, marrón
bruise (n) morado m
brush cepillo m
Brussels Bruselas
bucket balde, cubo m
buffet car coche
  comedor
buggy cochecito de niño
build construir
building edificio m
bulb (light) lamparilla f
bulb (plant) bulbo m
bumper
  guardabarros m
bun magdalena f
bunch manojo m
bureau de change
  oficina de cambio
burglar ladrón/
  ladrona m/f
burglary robo m
burn quemar
burst explotar
bus autobús m
bus stop
  parada de autobús
bush arbusto m
business negocios mpl
business trip
  viaje de negocios

busy ocupado/a
but pero
butcher carnicero/a m/f
butter mantequilla f
butterfly mariposa f
button botón m
buy comprar
by por
bypass (road)
  desviación, carretera de
  circunvalación

C

cab taxi m
cabbage repollo m
cabin cabina f
cable car teleférico m
cake pastel m, tarta f
cake shop pastelería f
calculator calculadora f
calf ternera f
call (n) llamada f
call (vb) llamar
calm calma
camp (vb) acampar
camp site
  campamento m
can (n) lata f
can (vb) poder
can opener
  abridor de latas
Canada Canadá
canal canal m
cancel cancelar
cancellation
  cancelación f
cancer cáncer m
candle vela f

candy dulce m
canoe canoa f
cap gorro m
capital (city) capital f
capital (money)
   capital m
car coche, carro, auto m
car ferry transbordador
   de coches
car hire alquiler de
   coches
car insurance
   seguro de coche
car keys
   llaves del coche
car parts partes del
   coche
car wash lavado de
   coches
caravan remolque m
caravan site
   campamento de
   remolques
carburettor
   carburador m
card carta f, tarjeta f
cardboard cartón m
cardigan rebeca f
careful cuidado
caretaker portero/a m/f
carpenter
   carpintero/a m/f
carpet alfombra f
carriage vagón m
carrier bag bolsa f
carrot zanahoria f
carry cargar
carry-cot cuna portable

carton caja f
case caso m
cash efectivo, dinero
   efectivo
cash desk caja f
cash dispenser
   cajero automático
cash register caja f
cashier cajero/a m/f
cassette cassette f
castle castillo m
casualty department
   urgencias
cat gato/a m/f
catch coger, agarrar
cathedral catedral f
Catholic (adj, n)
   católico/a m/f
cauliflower coliflor f
cave cueva f
CD player centro
   musical, toca discos
ceiling cielo raso
celery apio m
cellar bodega f
cemetery cementerio m
Centigrade centígrado
centimetre
   centímetro m
central heating
   calefacción central
central locking
   bloqueo automático
centre centro m
century siglo m
certain certeza
certainly ciertamente,
   claro

ENGLISH → SPANISH

certificate certificado m
chair silla f
chair lift elevador
 de silla
chambermaid
 camarera f
champagne champán m
change (n) cambio m
change (vb) cambiar
changing room
 vestuario m
channel canal m
chapel capilla f
charcoal carbón m
charge cargar
charge card
 tarjeta de crédito
charter flight
 vuelo chárter
cheap barato/a
cheap rate
 precio barato
cheaper más barato
check registrar
check in registrarse,
 inscribirse
cheek mejilla f
Cheers! ¡Salud!
cheese queso m
chef cocinero/a m/f
chemist
 farmacéutico/a m/f
cheque cheque m
cheque book
 libreta de cheques
cheque card tarjeta de
 identidad bancario
cherry cereza f

chess ajedrez m
chest pecho m
chest of drawers
 cómoda f
chestnut castaño m
chewing gum goma de
 mascar, chicle m
chicken pollo m
chicken pox varicela f
child niño/a, chico/a,
 chaval/a m/f
child car seat asiento
 de coche para niños
chimney chimenea f
chin barbilla f, mentón m
China China
china porcelana f
chips patatas fritas,
 papas fritas fpl
chives cebolleta f
chocolate chocolate m
chocolates
 bombones mpl
choir coro m
choose escoger, elegir
chop cortar
Christian name
 nombre de pila
Christmas Navidad f
Christmas Eve
 Nochebuena f
church iglesia f
cider sidra f
cigar puro m
cigarette cigarrillo m
cigarette lighter
 mechero m,
 encendedor m

cinema cine m
circle círculo m
cistern cisterna f
citizen ciudadano/a m/f
city ciudad f
city centre centro de la
  ciudad
class clase f
clean (adj) limpio/a
clean (vb) limpiar
cleaning solution
  detergente m
cleansing lotion
  crema limpiadora
clear (adj) claro/a
clever listo/a, inteligente
client cliente m/f
cliff acantilado m
climate clima m
climb subir
cling film plástico para
  envolver
clinic clínica f
cloakroom baño m,
  servicios mpl
clock reloj m
closed cerrado/a
cloth paño m
clothes ropas fpl
clothes line
  tendedero m
clothes peg broches
  para la ropa, pinza f
clothing ropa f
cloud nube f
clutch (car)
  embrague m
coach autocar m

coal carbón m
coast costa f
coastguard guardia
  costera
coat abrigo m
coat hanger
  percha para abrigo
cockroach cucaracha f
cocoa cacao m
coconut coco m
cod bacalao m
code código m
coffee café m
coil (n, contraceptive)
  espiral f
coil (n, rope) rollo m
coin moneda f
Coke Coca Cola f
colander colador m
cold frío/a
collapse (vb)
  derrumbarse
collar cuello m
collarbone clavícula f
colleague colega m/f
collect recoger
collect call llamada a
  cobro revertido
colour color m
colour blind
  daltónico/a
colour film film a color
comb (n) peine m
comb (vb) peinar
come venir
come back volver,
  regresar
come in entre

comedy comedia f
comfortable cómodo/a
company compañía f
compartment
compartimento m
compass compás m
complain quejarse
complaint queja f
completely
completamente,
totalmente
composer
compositor/a m/f
compulsory
obligatorio/a
computer ordenador m,
computadora f
concert concierto m
concession concesión f
concussion
conmoción cerebral
condition condición f
condom preservativo,
condón m
conference
conferencia f
confirm confirmar
confirmation
confirmación f
confused confundido/a
Congratulations!
¡Enhorabuena!
¡Felicitaciones!
connecting flight
vuelo de conexión
connection (elec)
conexión f

connection (phone)
instalación f
conscious conciente
constipated estreñido/a
consulate consulado m
contact contacto m
contact lenses
lentes de contacto
continue continuar
contraceptive
anticonceptivo m/f
contract contrato m
convenient
conveniente
cook (n) cocinero/a m/f
cook (vb) cocinar
cooker cocina f,
hornillo m
cookie galleta f
cooking utensils
utensillos de cocina
cool fresco/a
cool bag, cool box
nevera portátil
copy copiar
cork corcho m
corkscrew
sacacorcho m
corner esquina f
correct (adj) correcto/a
corridor pasillo m
cost coste, costo m
cot cuna f
cotton algodón m
cotton wool
algodón hidrófilo
couch sofá m
couchette litera f

cough (n) tos f
cough (vb) toser
cough mixture
jarabe para la tos
Could I? ¿Podría?
¿Puedo?
couldn't no puedo
counter mostrador m
country país m
countryside
campo m, afueras
couple pareja f
courier service servicio
de entrega/courier
course curso m
cousin primo/a m/f
cover charge entrada f
cow vaca f
crab cangrejo m
craft artesanía f
cramp calambre m
crash (vb) chocar
crash helmet casco m
crazy loco/a
cream crema f
crèche guardería de
niños
credit card tarjeta
de crédito
crime delito m
crisps patatas fritas,
papas fritas fpl
crockery loza f
cross (n) cruz m
cross (vb) cruzar
crossing cruce m
crossroads cruce de
caminos

crossword puzzle
crucigrama m
crowd muchedumbre f
crowded lleno/a,
repleto/a
crown corona f
cruise crucero m
crutches muletas fpl
cry llorar
cucumber pepino m
cufflinks gemelos mpl
cup taza f, pocillo m
cupboard armario m,
ropero m
curly rizado/a
currency moneda f
current (n) corriente f
curtain cortina f
cushion almohadón m
custard natillas fpl,
crema pastelera
custom costumbre f
customer cliente m/f
customs aduana f
cut cortar
cutlery cubertería f
cycle (vb) montar/
andar en bicicleta
cycle track sendero de
bicicletas
cyst quiste m
cystitis cistitis f
Czech Republic
República Checa

D
daily diariamente
damage daño m

ENGLISH → SPANISH

damp humedad f
dance (vb) bailar
danger peligro m
dangerous peligroso/a
dark oscuro/a
date (appointment) cita f
date (fruit) dátil m
date (of year) fecha f
date of birth fecha de nacimiento
daughter hija f
daughter-in-law nuera f
dawn (n) alba f, amanecer m
day día m
dead muerto/a
deaf sordo/a
deal trato m
dear querido/a
death muerte f
debts deudas fpl
decaffeinated descafeinado/a
December diciembre m
decide decidir
decision decisión f
deck chair silla de patio, tumbona f
deduct descontar
deep profundo/a
definitely definitiva-mente, por supuesto
degree (measure-ment) grado
degree (qualification) título
delay demora f

deliberately deliberadamente
delicious delicioso/a, rico/a
deliver entregar
delivery entrega f
Denmark Dinamarca
dental floss hilo dental
dentist dentista m/f
dentures dentaduras
depart salir
department sección f
department store grandes almacenes mpl, tienda de departamentos
departure salida f
departure lounge sala de embarque
deposit depósito m
describe describir
description descripción f
desert desierto m
desk escritorio m
dessert postre m
destination destino m
details datos, detalles mpl
detergent detergente m
detour desvío m
develop desarrollar
diabetic (adj, n) diabético/a m/f
dial (vb) marcar
dialling code prefijo m

dialling tone señal de marcar
diamond diamante m
diaper pañal m
diarrhoea diarrea f
diary agenda f, diario m
dice dados mpl
dictionary diccionario m
die morir
diesel diesel m
diet dieta f
difference diferencia f
different diferente
difficult difícil
dinghy bote m, lancha neumática
dining room comedor m
dinner cena f
direct (adj) directo/a
direction dirección f
dirty sucio/a
disabled inválido/a
disappear desaparecer
disappointed decepcionado/a
disaster desastre m
disconnected desconectado
discount descuento m
discover descubrir
disease enfermedad f
dish plato m
dishtowel trapo de cocina
dishwasher lavaplatos m
disinfectant desinfectante m

disk disco m
disposable diapers/ nappies pañales descartables
distance distancia f
district barrio m, distrito m
disturb molestar
dive bucear
diving board trampolín m
divorced divorciado
DIY shop ferretería f
dizzy mareado/a
do hacer
doctor médico/a m/f
document documento m
dog perro/a m/f
doll muñeca f
domestic doméstico/a
door puerta f
doorbell timbre m
doorman portero m
double doble
double bed cama doble
double room habitación doble
doughnut donut m, rosquilla f
downhill cuesta abajo, barranca abajo
downstairs abajo
dozen docena f
drain (n) desagüe m
draught corriente f
draught beer cerveza de barril/tirada

ENGLISH → SPANISH

ENGLISH → SPANISH

drawer cajón m
drawing dibujo m
dreadful horrible
dress vestido m
dressing (bandage) vendaje m
dressing (salad) aliño m, vinagreta f
dressing gown bata f
drill (n) taladro m
drink (n) bebida f
drink (vb) beber
drinking water agua potable
drive conducir, manejar
driver conductor/a m/f, chófer m
driving licence carnet de conducir, licencia de conductor
drop (n) gota f
drug (medicine) medicamento m
drug (narcotic) droga f
drunk (adj, n) borracho/a m/f
dry seco/a
dry cleaner's tintorería f
dryer secadora f
duck pato/a m/f
due pagadero/a
dull apagado/a, pesado/a
dummy chupete m
during durante
dust polvo m
dustbin cubo de la basura
duster paño m, trapo m

dustpan recogedor m
Dutch, Dutchman, Dutchwoman (adj, n) holandés/holandesa m/f
duty-free libre de impuestos
duvet edredón m
duvet cover funda para edredón
dye (n) tinte m
dye (vb) teñir, colorear
dynamo dínamo f

E

each cada
eagle águila f
ear oído m
earache dolor de oídos
earphones auriculares mpl
earrings pendientes, aros mpl
earth tierra f
earthquake terremoto m
east este m
Easter Semana Santa
Easter egg huevo de pascua
easy fácil
eat comer
EC Comunidad Europea
economy economía f
economy class clase económica
edge borde m
eel anguila f
egg huevo m

either ... or o ... o
elastic elástico/a
elbow codo m
electric eléctrico/a
electrician
  electricista m/f
electricity electricidad f
elevator elevador,
  asecensor m
embassy embajada f
emergency
  emergencia f
emergency exit salida
  de emergencia
empty vacío/a
end final m
engaged (occupied)
  ocupado/a
**engaged (to be
  married)**
  comprometido/a
engine motor m
engineer ingeniero/a m/f
England Inglaterra
English (language)
  inglés
English Channel Canal
  de la Mancha
**English, Englishman/
  woman (adj, n)**
  inglés/inglesa m/f
enjoy disfrutar
enlargement
  ampliación f
enough suficiente
enquiry informe m,
  investigación f

enquiry desk
  mostrador de
  información
enter entrar
entrance entrada f
entrance fee entrada f
envelope sobre m
epilepsy epilepsia f
epileptic epiléptico/a
equipment equipo m
error error m
escalator escalera
  mecánica
escape (vb) escapar
especially
  especialmente
essential esencial
estate agent agente
  inmobilario/a
Estonia Estonia
EU Unión Europea
Europe Europa
European (adj, n)
  europeo/a m/f
even (adj) parejo/a,
  uniforme
even (adv) hasta
evening tarde f, (early),
  noche f (late)
eventually finalmente
every cada
everyone cada uno,
  todos/todas m/f
everything todo
everywhere por todas
  partes
exactly exactamente
examination examen m

ENGLISH → SPANISH

ENGLISH → SPANISH

example, for example
ejemplo m, por ejemplo
excellent excelente
except excepto
excess luggage
exceso de equipaje
exchange (n) cambio,
intercambio m
exciting entusiasmante
exclude excluir
excursion excursión f
excuse (n) disculpa f
Excuse me! ¡Perdón!
exhaust pipe tubo
de escape
exhausted agotado/a
exhibition exposición f
exit salida f
expect esperar
expenses gastos mpl
expensive caro/a
experienced
con experiencia,
experimentado/a
expire caducar, vencer
explain explicar
explosion explosión f
export exportar
exposure exposición f,
revelación f
express (train)
expreso m
extension extensión f
extension lead cable
de extensión
extra extra
extraordinary
extraordinario/a

eye ojo m
eye drops
gotas para los ojos
eye make-up remover
desmaquillador para
ojos
eye shadow sombra
de ojos

F
fabric tejido m
façade fachada f
face cara f
factory fábrica f
faint (vb) desmayarse
fair (fête) feria f
fair (hair colour)
rubio/a
fair (just) justo/a
fairly bastante
fake (adj) falso/a
fake (vb) simular
fall caer
false falso/a
family familia f
famous famoso/a
fan ventilador m
fanbelt correa del
ventilador
far (adj) lejano/a
far (adv) lejos
fare tarifa f
farm granja f
farmer granjero/a m/f
farmhouse cortijo m,
hacienda f
fashionable de moda
fast rápido/a

fasten abrochar, ajustar
fasten seatbelt ajustar el cinturón de seguridad
fat gordo/a
father padre m
father-in-law suegro m
fatty graso/a
fault defecto m, culpa f
faulty defectuoso/a
favourite favorito/a
fax facsímil
February febrero m
feed (vb) alimentar
feel sentir
feet pies mpl
female mujer f
fence alambrada f
fender parachoques m, guardabarros m
ferry transbordador m, ferry m
festival festival m
fetch buscar, traer
fever fiebre f
few, a few pocos/as m/f
fiancé, fiancée novio/a, prometido/a m/f
field campo m
fight (n) pelea, lucha f
fight (vb) luchar, pelear
file (folder) archivo m, carpeta f
file (tool) lima f
fill, fill in, fill up llenar
fillet filete m
filling (sandwich) relleno m

filling (tooth) empaste m
film (n) película f
film (vb) filmar
film processing revelado
filter filtro m
filthy mugriento/a
find encontrar
fine (adj) fino/a
fine (n) multa f
finger dedo m
finish (vb) terminar
fire fuego m
fire brigade bomberos mpl
fire exit salida de emergencia
fire extinguisher extintor de fuego
first, at first primero/a, al principio
first aid primeros auxilios
first-aid kit maletín de primeros auxilios
first class primera clase
first floor primer piso m
first name primer nombre, nombre de pila
fish pescado m
fishing permit permiso de pesca
fishing rod caña de pescar
fishmonger's pescadería f

ENGLISH → SPANISH

fit (healthy) en forma
fitting room cambiador m
fix arreglar, reparar
fizzy con gas
flannel franela f
flash (of lightning) relámpago
flashlight linterna eléctrica
flask termo m
flat (n) apartamento m, piso m
flat battery batería descargada
flat tyre neumático sin aire
flavour sabor m
flaw desperfecto m, imperfección f
flea pulga f
flight vuelo m
flip flops chancletas fpl
flippers aletas fpl
flood inundación f
floor (of room) suelo m
floor (storey) piso m
floorcloth trapo/paño para el suelo
florist florista m/f
flour harina f
flower flor f
flu gripe f
fluent con fluidez
fly (vb) volar
fog niebla, neblina f
folk gente f
follow seguir

food alimento m, comida f
food poisoning comida envenenada
food shop almacén m, tienda f
foot pie m
football fútbol m
football match partido/ juego de fútbol
footpath sendero m
for por, para
forbidden prohibido/a
forehead frente f
foreign raro/a
foreign, foreigner (adj, n) extranjero/a m/f
forest bosque m
forget olvidar
fork tenedor m
form (document) formulario m
form (shape) forma f
formal formal, educado/a
fortnight quincena f
fortress fuerte m
fortunately por suerte
fountain fuente f
four-wheel drive cuatro por cuatro
fox zorro/a m/f
fracture fractura f
frame marco m
France Francia
free libre
freelance por su cuenta, independiente
freeway autopista f

freezer congelador m
**French, Frenchman/
  woman (adj, n)**
  francés/francesa m/f
French fries patatas
  fritas, papas fritas fpl
frequent frecuente
fresh fresco/a
Friday viernes m
fridge nevera f,
  refrigerador m
fried frito/a
friend amigo/a m/f
friendly amigable,
  simpático/a
frog rana f
from (origin) de
from (time) desde
front frente m
frost helada f
frozen congelado/a
fruit fruta f
fruit juice zumo/jugo
  de fruta
fry freír
frying pan sartén f
fuel gasolina f,
  combustible m
fuel gauge indicador
  de la gasolina
full lleno/a
full board pensión
  completa
fun (adj) divertido/a
fun (n) diversión f
funeral funeral m
funicular funicular m
funny gracioso/a

fur piel f
fur coat abrigo de piel
furnished amueblado
furniture muebles mpl
further más allá
fuse fusible m
fuse box
  caja de fusibles
future futuro m

G
Gallery galería f
gallon galón m
game juego m
garage garaje m
garden jardín m
garlic ajo m
gas gas, combustible m
gas cooker hornalla f,
  estufilla f
gate puerta f
gay gay, homosexual
gay bar bar gay
gear equipo m, ropa f
gear lever palanca
  de cambios
gearbox caja de
  cambios
general general
generous generoso/a
Geneva Ginebra
gents' toilet servicio
  de caballeros, baño
  de hombres
genuine auténtico/a,
  genuino/a, real
German (adj, n)
  alemán, alemana m/f

ENGLISH → SPANISH

German measles
  rubeola f
Germany Alemania
get obtener
get off bajar
get on subir
get up levantarse
gift regalo m
girl niña f
girlfriend novia f
give dar
give back devolver
glacier glaciar m
glad encantado/a
glass (tumbler) vaso m
glasses (spectacles)
  lentes m/f, gafas fpl,
  anteojos mpl
gloomy apagado/a
gloves guantes mpl
glue pegamento m
go ir
go (by car) ir/andar
  conducir, ir/andar
  manejar
go (on foot) andar
go away irse
go back volver
goat cabra f
God Dios m
goggles gafas
  protectoras
gold oro m
golf club (place) club
  de golf
golf club (stick) palo
  de golf

golf course campo
  de golf
good bueno/a
good afternoon
  buenas tardes
good day buenos días
good evening buenas
  tardes (if still light)
Good Friday Viernes
  Santo
good luck buena suerte
good morning
  buenos días
good night
  buenas noches
goodbye adiós
goose ganso m
Gothic gótico/a
government gobierno m
gradually poco a poco,
  gradualmente
gram gramo m
grammar gramática f
grand grandioso/a
granddaughter nieta f
grandfather abuelo m
grandmother abuela f
grandparents
  abuelos mpl
grandson nieto m
grapes uvas fpl
grass césped m
grated rallado/a
grateful agradecido/a
gravy salsa f
greasy graso/a
great gran, grande,
  vasto/a, importante

Great Britain
Gran Bretaña
Greece Grecia
Greek (adj, n)
griego/a m/f
green verde
greengrocer's
verdulería
greeting saludo m
grey gris
grilled a la parrilla
ground tierra f
ground floor
planta baja
group grupo m
guarantee garantía f
guard guardia m/f
guest huésped/a m/f
guesthouse pensión f
guide guía m/f
guide book
guía de turismo
guided tour
visita guiada
guitar guitarra f
gun arma f
gym gimnasio m

H
hail granizo m
hair cabello m, pelo m
hairbrush
cepillo de pelo
haircut corte de pelo
hairdresser
peluquero/a m/f
hairdresser's
peluquería f

hairdryer secador
de pelo
half (adj) medio/a,
half (n) mitad f
hall sala f
ham jamón m
hamburger
hamburguesa f
hammer martillo m
hand mano f
hand luggage
equipaje de mano
handbag bolso m,
cartera f
handbrake
freno de mano
handicapped
minusválido/a
handkerchief pañuelo m
handle mango m,
palanca f
handmade
hecho a mano
handsome guapo/a
hang up (phone)
colgar
hanger percha f
hang-gliding vuelo libre,
aladeltismo
hangover resaca f
happen pasar
happy feliz
Happy Easter!
¡Feliz Semana Santa!
Happy New Year!
¡Feliz Año Nuevo!
harbour puerto m
hard duro/a

ENGLISH → SPANISH

107

ENGLISH → SPANISH

hard disk disco duro
hardly apenas
hardware shop
ferretería f
harvest cosecha f
hat sombrero m
have tener
have to deber,
tener que
hay fever
fiebre del heno
hazelnut avellana f
he él
head cabeza f
headache
dolor de cabeza
headlight/s faro m,
luces delanteras
headphones
auriculares mpl
health food shop
tienda de alimentos
naturales
healthy saludable
hear oír, escuchar
hearing aid audífono m
heart corazón m
heart attack
ataque al corazón
heartburn acedía f
heat calor m
heater calefactor m
heating calefacción f
heavy pesado/a
heel talón m
height altura f
helicopter helicóptero m
helmet casco m

Help! ¡Ayuda!
help (vb) ayudar
hem dobladillo m, orilla f
her su
herbal tea té de
hierbas, té natural
herbs hierbas fpl
here aquí, acá
hernia hernia f
hide esconder
high alto/a
high blood pressure
presión alta (sangre)
high chair silla alta
him, to him él, a él
hip cadera f
hip replacement
reemplazo de cadera
hire (vb) alquilar
hire car coche de
alquiler
his su
historic histórico/a
history historia f
hit golpear
hitchhike hacer
autostop, hacer dedo
hold tener
hole hueco m, hoyo m,
agujero m
holidays vacaciones fpl
holy sagrado/a
home casa f
homesickness
echar de menos
homosexual
homosexual
honest honrado/a

honey miel f
honeymoon
luna de miel
hood (car) capó/
capota m/f
hood (garment)
capucha f
hope esperanza f
hopefully ojalá
horn (animal) cuerno m
horn (car) bocina f
horse caballo m
horse racing
carrera de caballos
horse riding
paseo a caballo
hose pipe manguera f
hospital hospital m
hospitality hospitalidad f
hostel parador m,
albergue **m**
hot caliente
hot spring termas fpl
hot-water bottle
bolsa de agua caliente
hour hora f
hourly (adj) cada hora
hourly (adv) por horas
house casa f
house wine
vino de la casa
housework trabajo
doméstico, tarea **f**
hovercraft
hidrodeslizador m
How? ¿Cómo?
How are you?
¿Cómo estás?

How do you do?
¿Qué tal? ¿Cómo
estás?
How many?
¿Cuánto/a?
How much is it?
¿Cuánto es?
humid húmedo/a
humour humor m
Hungarian (adj, n)
húngaro/a **m/f**
Hungary Hungría
hungry con hambre
hunt cazar
hunting permit
permiso de caza
hurry (vb) darse prisa
hurt (vb) doler
hurts duele
husband marido,
esposo m
hydrofoil hidroala f
hypodermic needle
aguja hipodérmica

I
I yo
ice hielo m
ice cream helado m
ice rink pista de hielo
ice skates patines mpl
iced coffee café
helado **m**
idea idea f
identity card carné de
identidad, tarjeta de
identidad, documento
de identidad

ENGLISH → SPANISH

if si
if not si no
ignition encendido **m**
ignition key
  llave de contacto, llave
  de encendido
ill enfermo/a
illness enfermedad **f**
immediately
  inmediatamente
important importante
impossible imposible
improve mejorar
in en
inch pulgada **f**
included incluido
inconvenience
  inconveniente **f**
incredible increíble
Indian (adj, n)
  indio/a **m/f**
indicator indicador
  de giro, intermitente **m**
indigestion indigestión **f**
indoor pool piscina
  climatizada/cubierta
indoors a puertas
  adentro
infection infección **f**
infectious infeccioso/a
inflammation
  inflamación **f**
inflate inflar
informal informal
information
  información **f**
ingredients
  ingredientes **mpl**

injection inyección **f**
injured lastimado/a,
  herido/a
injury herida **f**
ink tinta **f**
in-laws suegros **mpl**
inn posada **f**
inner tube tubo interno,
  cámara de aire
insect insecto **m**
insect bite
  picadura de insecto
insect repellent
  repelente de insectos
inside dentro, adentro
insist insistir
insomnia insomnio **m**
inspect registrar
instant coffee
  café instantáneo
instead en lugar de
insulin insulina **f**
insurance seguro **m**
intelligent inteligente
intend significar
interesting interesante
international
  internacional
interpreter
  intérprete **m/f**
intersection cruce **m**
interval intervalo **m**
into en
introduce introducir,
  presentar (people)
investigation
  investigación **f**
invitation invitación **f**

invite invitar
invoice factura f
Ireland Irlanda
Irish, Irishman/woman (adj, n) irlandés/ irlandesa m/f
iron (n, appliance) plancha f
iron (n, metal) hierro m
iron (vb) planchar
ironing board tabla de planchar
ironmonger's ferretería f
is es/está
island isla f
it (direct object) lo/la
it (indirect object) le
it (subject) él/ella/ello
Italian (adj, n) italiano/a m/f
Italian (language) italiano
Italy Italia
itch (n) picor m
itch (vb) picar

J

jack (car) gato m
jacket chaqueta f, abrigo m
jam jalea f, mermelada f
jammed tapado
January enero m
jar frasco m
jaundice ictericia f
jaw mandíbula f
jealous celoso/a

jelly jalea f
jellyfish medusa, aguamala f
jersey jersey m
Jew, Jewish (n, adj) judío/a m/f
jeweller's joyería f
jewellery joyas fpl
job trabajo m
jog (n) trote m
jog (vb) correr, trotar
join unirse, asociarse
joint juntura f
joke broma f
journey travesía f, viaje m
joy alegría f
judge juez m/f
jug jarra f
juice zumo m, jugo m
July julio m
jump (n) salto m
jump (vb) saltar
jump leads cables de conexion de batería
jumper súeter, jersey m
junction cruce m
June junio m
just (fair) justo/a
just (only) solamente

K

keep guardar
Keep the change! ¡Guarde el cambio!
kettle hervidor m
key llave f
key ring llavero m
kick patear

ENGLISH → SPANISH

kidney riñón m
kill matar
kilo kilo m
kilogram kilogramo m
kilometre kilómetro m
kind amable
king rey m
kiosk quiosco m
kiss (n) beso m
kiss (vb) besar
kitchen cocina f
kitchenette cocinilla f
knee rodilla f
knickers bragas fpl
knife cuchillo m
knit tejer
knitting needle
   aguja de tejer
knitwear tejido m
knock golpear
knock down derribar
knock over atropellar
know saber, conocer

L
label etiqueta f
lace puntilla f
ladder escalera f
ladies' toilet
   servicio de damas,
   baño de mujeres
ladies' wear
   ropa de mujer
lady dama f, mujer f,
   señora f
lager cerveza rubia
lake lago m
lamb cordero m

lamp lámpara f
land tierra f
landlady propietaria f
landlord propietario m
landslide
   desprendimiento
   de tierras
lane carril m
language lengua f,
   idioma m
language course
   curso de idioma
large gran, grande
last último/a
last night anoche
late tarde
later luego, más tarde
Latvia Latvia
laugh (n) risa f
laugh (vb) reír
launderette,
   laundromat
   lavandería automática
laundry lavandería f
lavatory servicios mpl,
   baño m
law ley f
lawyer abogado/a m/f
laxative (adj, n)
   laxante m
lazy perezoso/a, vago/a
lead (n, metal) plomo
lead (vb) llevar
lead-free sin plomo
leaf hoja f
leaflet folleto m
leak (n) agujero m
leak (vb) gotear

learn aprender
lease (n) contrato de alquiler
lease (vb) arrendar
leather piel f, cuero m
leave salir, dejar
leek puerro m
left, to the left izquierdo/a, a la izquierda
left-hand drive conducción a la izquierda
left-handed zurdo/a
leg pierna f
lemon limón m
lemonade limonada f
lend prestar
lens lente f
lenses lentes m/f
lentil lenteja f
lesbian (adj, n) lesbiana f
less menos
lesson lección f, clase f
let (vb, allow) dejar, permitir
let (vb, hire) alquilar
letter carta f
letterbox buzón m
lettuce lechuga f
level crossing cruce a nivel
lever palanca f
library biblioteca f
licence licencia f, permiso m
lid tapa f

lie (n, untruth) mentira f
lie (vb, fib) mentir
lie down acostarse
life vida f
life belt cinturón salvavidas
life insurance seguro de vida
life jacket chaleco salvavidas
lifeguard socorrista m/f
lift (n, elevator) elevador, ascensor m
lift (vb) levantar
light (adj, colour) claro/a
light (adj, weight) ligero/a, liviano/a
light (n) luz f
light (vb) iluminar
light bulb bombilla f, lamparilla f
lightning rayo m
like (prep) como
like (vb) gustar
lime lima f
line línea f
linen lino m
lingerie ropa interior
lion león m
lipstick lápiz de labios
liqueur licor m
list lista f
listen escuchar
Lithuania Lituania
litre litro m
litter (n) basura f
litter (vb) ensuciar

ENGLISH → SPANISH

ENGLISH → SPANISH

little pequeño/a
live vivir
lively vivo/a
liver hígado m
living room sala de estar
loaf barra f
lobby vestíbulo m
lobster langosta f
local local
lock (n) cerradura f
lock (vb) cerrar
lock in guardar en el armario
lock out cerrar, dejar encerrado
locked in bajo llave
locker armario m
lollipop pirulí, chupón
long (adj, size) largo/a
long (adj, time) mucho/a
long-distance call llamada de larga distancia
look after cuidar
look at mirar
look for buscar
look forward to esperar con ilusión
loose suelto/a
lorry camioneta f
lose perder
lost perdido/a
lost property propiedad perdida
lot mucho/a
loud ruidoso/a

lounge sala de estar, salón m
love (n) amor m
love (vb) amar
lovely precioso/a
low bajo/a
low fat bajas calorías
luck suerte f
luggage equipaje m
luggage rack portaequipaje m
luggage tag etiqueta f
luggage trolley carrito para equipaje
lump terrón m, trozo m
lunch almuerzo m
lung pulmón m
Luxembourg Luxemburgo
luxury lujo m

M

machine máquina f
mad loco/a
made hecho/a
magazine revista f
maggot gusano m
magnet imán m
magnifying glass lupa f
maid criada f
maiden name nombre de soltera
mail (n) correo m
mail (vb) enviar por correo
main principal
main course plato principal

main post office
correo central
main road
calle principal/mayor
mains switch
interruptor principal
make hacer
male masculino
man hombre m
man-made fibre
fibra sintética
manager gerente m/f
manual (adj, n)
manual m
many muchos/as
map mapa m
marble mármol m
March marzo m
market mercado m
marmalade mermelada f
married casado/a
marsh pantano m
mascara rímel m
mashed potatoes
puré de patatas/papas
mask máscara f
Mass (rel) misa f
mast mástil m
match (sport) partido m
matches (for lighting)
fósforos mpl
material tejido m
matter asunto m
matter – it doesn't
matter no importa
mattress colchón f
May mayo m
may poder

maybe quizás, tal vez
mayonnaise mayonesa f
me me
meal comida f
mean (intend) significar
mean (nasty) malo/a
measles sarampión m
measure (n) medida f
measure (vb) medir
meat carne f
mechanic
mecánico/a m/f
medical insurance
seguro médico
medicine (drug)
medicamento m
medicine (science)
medicina f
medieval medieval
Mediterranean
mediterráneo/a
medium mediano/a
medium dry wine
vino medio seco
medium rare (meat)
carne medio hecha
medium sized
talla media
meet encontrar
meeting reunión f
melon melón m
melt derretir
men hombres
mend remendar
meningitis meningitis
menswear
ropa de hombre
mention mencionar

ENGLISH → SPANISH

menu menú m
meringue merengue m
message recado m
metal metal m
meter contador m
metre metro m
metro metro m
microwave oven
  micro ondas m
midday mediodía m
middle medio m
midnight medianoche f
might (vb) poder
migraine migraña f
mile milla f
milk leche f
minced meat
  carne picada
mind mente f
mineral water
  agua mineral
minister ministro/a m/f
mint menta f
minute minuto m
mirror espejo m
Miss señorita f
missing perdido/a,
  desaparecido/a
mist neblina f
mistake error m
misunderstanding
  malentendido m
mix (vb) mezclar
mix-up (n) confusión f
mix up (vb) confundir
mobile phone
  teléfono móvil

moisturizer
  crema hidratante
moment momento m
monastery monasterio m
Monday lunes m
money dinero m
money belt monedero m
money order giro m
month mes m
monthly mensualmente
monument
  monumento m
moon luna f
mooring amarradero m
more más
morning mañana f
mosque mezquita f
mosquito mosquito m
most la mayoría de
mostly generalmente
moth polilla f
mother madre f
mother-in-law suegra f
motor motor m
motorbike motocicleta f
motorboat lancha f
motorway autopista f
mountain montaña f
mountain rescue
  rescate de montaña
mountaineering
  montañismo m
mouse ratón m
moustache bigote m
mouth boca f
mouth ulcer
  úlcera de boca

mouthwash
desinfectante bucal
move mover,
move house mudarse
de casa
Mr señor m
Mrs señora f
Ms señorita f
much mucho/a
mud lodo, barro m
mug tazón m
mugged robado
mumps paperas fpl
muscle músculo m
museum museo m
mushroom hongo m,,
champiñon m
musician músico/a m/f
Muslim musulmán/
musulmana m/f
mussel mejillón m
must deber
mustard mostaza f
mutton cordero m
my mi
myself yo mismo

N
nail uña f
nail brush cepillo
de uñas
nail file lima de uñas
nail polish/varnish
pintura de uñas, esmalte
de uñas
nail polish remover
quitaesmalte

nail scissors
tijeras para uñas
name nombre m
nanny niñera f
napkin servilleta f
nappy pañal m
narrow angosto/a,
estrecho/a
nasty malo/a, sucio/a,
indecente
national nacional
nationality nacionalidad f
natural natural
nature naturaleza f
nature reserve
reserva natural
nausea náusea f
navy armada f
navy blue azul marino
near (adj) cercano/a
near (adv) cerca
nearby (adj) cercano/a
nearby (adv) cerca, en
los alrededores
nearly casi
necessary necesario/a
neck cuello m
necklace collar m
need (n) necesidad f
need (vb) necesitar
needle aguja f
negative (n, photo)
negativo m
neighbour vecino/a m/f
neither ... nor ni ... ni
nephew sobrino m
nest nido m
net red f

Netherlands Países Bajos

never nunca

new nuevo/a

New Year Año Nuevo

New Year's Eve Nochevieja f

New Zealand, New Zealander Nueva Zelanda, neocelandés

news noticias fpl

news stand quiosko m

newspaper periódico m

next próximo/a

nice agradable

niece sobrina f

night, last night noche f, anoche

nightdress vestido de noche

no no

nobody nadie

noise ruido m

noisy ruidoso/a

non-alcoholic sin alcohol

non-smoking no fumador/a

none ninguno/a

north norte m

North Sea Mar del Norte

Northern Ireland Irlanda del Norte

Norway Noruega

Norwegian (adj, n) noruego/a m/f

nose nariz f

not no

note nota f

notebook cuaderno m

notepaper papel de carta

nothing nada

nothing else nada más

noticeboard tablón de anuncios

novel novela f

November noviembre m

now ahora

nudist beach playa nudista

number número m

number plate matrícula f

nurse enfermero/a m/f

nursery (plants) vivero m

nursery school guardería infantil, jardín de infancia

nursery slope pistas para principiantes

nut nuez f

nut (for bolt) tornillo m

O

oak roble m

oar remo m

oats avena f

obtain obtener

occasionally de vez en cuando

occupation ocupación f

occupied (e.g. toilet) ocupado/a

ocean océano m
October octubre m
odd (number) impar
odd (strange) raro/a
of de
off de
office oficina f
often con frecuencia
oil aceite m
ointment pomada f
OK bien, vale, pura vida
old viejo/a
old-age pensioner jubilado/a m/f
old-fashioned pasado/a de moda
olive aceituna f
olive oil aceite de oliva
omelette tortilla f
on en, sobre
once una vez
one uno m
one-way street calle de una sola mano
onion cebolla f
only (adj) solamente
only (adv) sólo
open abierto/a
open ticket billete abierto
opening times horario de apertura
opera ópera f
operation operación f
operator (phone) operador/a m/f
ophthalmologist oculista m/f

opposite opuesto/a
optician óptico/a m/f
or o
orange naranja f
orange juice zumo/jugo de naranja
orchestra orquesta f
order (n) orden m
order (vb) pedir
organic vegetables verduras orgánicas
other otro/a
otherwise de otra forma, si no
our nuestro/a
out fuera, afuera
out of order no funciona
outdoors al aire libre
outside fuera, afuera
outskirts afueras
oven horno m
ovenproof resistente al horno, refractario/a
over sobre
over here acá, aquí
over there allá
overcharge cobrar excesivamente
overcoat abrigo m
overdone muy hecho
overheat recalentar
overnight por la noche, durante la noche
overtake adelantar
owe deber
owl lechuza f

ENGLISH → SPANISH

ENGLISH → SPANISH

owner propietario/a, dueño/a **m/f**

P
pacemaker marcapasos **m**
pacifier chupete **m**
pack (vb) empacar
package paquete **m**
package holiday vacaciones organizadas
packet paquete **m**
padlock candado **m**
page página **f**
paid pagado/a
pail cubo **m**
pain dolor **m**
painful doloroso/a
painkiller mitigador, droga mitigadora, analgésico **m**
paint (vb) pintar
paint (n) pintura **f**
painting cuadro **m**
pair par **m**
palace palacio **m**
pale pálido/a
pan cacerola **f**
pancake crepe **f**
panties bragas **fpl**
pants pantalones **mpl**
pantyhose panty **m**
paper papel **m**
paper napkins servilletas de papel
parcel paquete **m**
Pardon? ¿Qué? ¿Disculpa?

parents padres **mpl**
parents-in-law suegros **mpl**
park (n) parque **m**
park (vb) aparcar
parking disc disco de aparcamiento
parking meter parquímetro **m**
parking ticket boleto de estacionamiento
part parte **f**
partner (companion) compañero/a **m/f**
partner (business) socio/a **m/f**
party (celebration) fiesta **f**
party (political) partido **m**
pass (vb) pasar
pass control control de pasaporte
passenger pasajero/a **m/f**
passport pasaporte **m**
past pasado **m**
pastry pastel **m**
path sendero **m**
patient (adj, n) paciente **m/f**
pattern patrón **m**
pavement calzada **f**
pay pagar
payment pago **m**
payphone teléfono pago/público

pea guisante m, chícharo m

peach melocotón m

peak pico m

peak rate precio de temporada alta

peanut cacahuete m, maní m

pear pera f

pearl perla f

peculiar peculiar

pedal pedal m

pedestrian peatón m

pedestrian crossing paso de peatones

peel (n) piel f

peel (vb) pelar

peg clavija f

pen lapicera, boli m

pencil lápiz m

penfriend amigo/a invisible, amigo/a por carta

peninsula península f

people gente f

pepper (vegetable) pimiento m

pepper (spice) pimienta f

per por

perfect perfecto/a

performance representación f

perfume perfume m

perhaps quizás, tal vez

period período m

perm permanente f

permit (n) permiso m

permit (vb) permitir

person persona f

pet animal doméstico

petrol combustible m, gasolina f

petrol can contenedor de gasolina

petrol station estación de servicio, gasolinera f

pharmacist farmacéutico/a m/f

pharmacy farmacia f

phone teléfono m

phone booth cabina telefónica

phone card tarjeta de llamadas

phone number número de teléfono

photo foto f

photocopy (n) fotocopia f

photograph (n) fotografía f

photograph (vb) fotografiar

phrase book libro de frases

piano piano m

pickpocket carterista f, ratero/a m/f

picnic picnic m, comida de campo

picture foto f

picture frame marco de foto

pie pastel m, empanada f

piece pieza f, pedazo m

ENGLISH → SPANISH

pig cerdo m, puerco m/f
pill pastilla f
pillow almohada f
pillowcase funda para almohada
pilot piloto m
pin alfiler m
pin number número de clave
pineapple piña f, ananá m
pink rosa m
pipe (plumbing) cañería f
pipe (smoking) pipa f
pity, It's a pity! pena f, ¡Qué pena!
place lugar m
plain simple
plait trenza f
plane avión m
plant planta f
plaster escayola f, yeso m
plastic plástico/a
plastic bag bolsa de plástico
plate plato m
platform plataforma f, andén m
play (n, theatre) obra f
play (vb, game) jugar
playground patio de recreo
please por favor
pleased encantado/a
Pleased to meet you! ¡Encantado!

plenty suficiente demasiado
pliers alicates mpl
plug (bath) tapón m
plug (elec) enchufe m
plum ciruela f
plumber plomero/a, fontanero/a m/f
p.m. (after noon) por la tarde
poached escalfado
pocket bolsillo m
point (n) punto m
point (vb) señalar
points (car) platinos mpl
poison veneno m
poisonous venenoso/a
Poland Polonia
Pole, Polish (n, adj) polaco/a m/f
police policía f
police station estación de policía, comisaría f
policeman/woman agente de policía
polish (n) cera f
polish (vb) pulir
polite respetuoso/a, educado/a
polluted contaminado
pool piscina f
poor (impecunious) pobre
poor (quality) malo/a
poppy amapola f
popular popular
population población f

pork carne de cerdo, carne de puerco
port (n, harbour) puerto m
port (n, wine) oporto m
porter portero/a m/f
portion porción, parte f
portrait retrato m
Portugal Portugal
Portuguese (adj, n) portugués/portuguesa m/f
posh elegante
possible posible
post (n) correo m
post (vb) enviar por correo
post office oficina de correos
post office box casilla de correo
postage franqueo m
postage stamp sello m, estampilla f
postal code código postal
postbox buzón m
postcard postal f
poster póster m
postman/postwoman cartero/a m/f
postpone aplazar
potato patata, papa f
pothole bache m
pottery cerámica f
pound libra f
pour servir
powder polvo m

powdered milk leche en polvo
power cut corte de electricidad
practice práctica f
practise practicar
pram cochecito m
prawn gamba f
pray rezar
prefer preferir
pregnant embarazada
prescription receta f
present (adj) presente
present (n) regalo m
present (vb) regalar
pressure presión f
pretty bonito/a
price precio m
priest cura m
prime minister primer/a ministro/a m/f
print (vb) imprimir
printed matter asunto escrito, impresos mpl
prison cárcel f
private privado/a
prize premio m
probably probablemente
problem problema m
programme, program programa m
prohibited prohibido/a
promise (n) promesa f
promise (vb) prometer
pronounce pronunciar
properly correctamente
Protestant protestante m/f

ENGLISH → SPANISH

public público/a
public holiday día feriado, fiesta nacional
pudding postre m
pull tirar
pullover jersey m, chaleco m
pump (vb) inflar
puncture pinchazo m
puppet show espectáculo de marionetas
purple morado/a
purse bolso m, monedero m
push empujar
pushchair silla de ruedas
put poner
put up with aguantar
pyjamas pijamas m

Q

quality calidad f
quantity cantidad f
quarantine cuarentena f
quarrel (n) riña f
quarrel (vb) pelear, discutir
quarter cuarto m
quay muelle m
queen reina f
question pregunta f, cuestión f
queue (n) cola f
queue (vb) hacer cola
quickly rápidamente
quiet tranquilo/a, quieto

quilt cobertor, edredón
quite completamente

R

rabbit conejo/a m/f
rabies rabia f
race (people) raza f
race (sport) carrera f
race course hipódromo m
racket raqueta f
radiator radiador m
radio radio f
radish rábano m
rag trapo m
railway ferrocarril m
railway station estación de tren, estación de ferrocarril
rain lluvia f
raincoat impermeable m
raisin pasa f
rake rastrillo m
rape (n) violación f
rape (vb) violar
rare raro/a
rash erupción m
raspberry frambuesa f
rat rata f
rate (of exchange) tipo de cambio
raw crudo/a
razor navaja de afeitar
razor blade hoja de afeitar
read leer
ready listo/a
real real

realize darse cuenta
really realmente
rear-view mirror espejo retrovisor
reasonable razonable
receipt recibo m
receiver (tax) recaudador/a m/f
receiver (telephone) auricular m
recently recientemente
reception recepción f
receptionist recepcionista m/f
recharge recargar
recipe receta f
recognize reconocer
recommend recomendar
record (n, legal) documento m
record (n, music) disco m
red rojo/a
red wine vino tinto
redcurrant grosella roja
reduce reducir
reduction reducción f
refund (n) reembolso m
refund (vb) devolver, reembolsar
refuse (n) basura f
refuse (vb) rechazar
region región f
register (n) registro m
register (vb) certificar

registered mail correo certificado
registration form formulario de inscripción
registration number número de inscripción
relative, relation pariente m/f
remain quedarse
remember recordar
rent (vb) alquilar
repair (n) reparación f
repair (vb) reparar
repeat repetir
reply (n) respuesta f
reply (vb) contestar
report (n) informe m
report (vb) informar
request (n) petición f, pedido m, solicitud f
request (vb) pedir
require requerir
rescue (n) rescate m
rescue salvar
reservation reserva f
reserve reservar
resident (adj, n) residente m/f
resort complejo turístico
rest (relax) descansar
rest (remainder) resto m
retired jubilado/a, retirado/a
return regresar, volver
return ticket billete de ida y vuelta
reverse (n) revés m

ENGLISH → SPANISH

ENGLISH → SPANISH

reverse (vb) dar marcha atrás
reverse gear marcha atrás
reverse-charge call llamada a cobro revertido
revolting asqueroso/a
rheumatism reuma m
rib costilla f
ribbon cinta f
rice arroz m
rich rico/a
ride montar
ridiculous ridículo/a
right derecho/a
right-hand drive conducción a la derecha
ring (n) anillo m
ring (vb) sonar
ring road camino circular
rip-off estafa f
ripe maduro/a
river río m
road calle f, camino m, carretera f
road accident accidente de tráfico
road map mapa de carreteras
road sign señal de tráfico
road works carretera en obras
roll darse vuelta
roof techo m
roof-rack portaequipaje m

room cuarto m, habitación f
rope soga, cuerda f
rose (flower) rosa f
rotten podrido/a
rough áspero/a
roughly aproximadamente
round redondo/a
roundabout rotonda f
row (n) fila f
row (vb) remar
royal real
rubber caucho m, goma f
rubbish basura f
rubella rubeola f
rudder timón m
rug alfombra f
ruin ruina f
ruler (for measuring) regla f
rum ron m
run correr
rush darse prisa
rusty oxidado/a
rye bread pan de centeno

S
sad triste
saddle silla de montar
safe (adj) seguro
safe (n) caja fuerte
safety belt cinturón de seguridad
safety pin imperdible m
sail navegar

sailing navegación f
salad ensalada f
salad dressing
  condimento para
  ensalada, vinagreta f
sale rebajas fpl
sales representative
  representante de ventas
salesperson
  vendedor/a m/f
salmon salmón m
salt sal f
same mismo/a, igual
sand arena f
sandals sandalias,
  ojotas fpl
sandwich bocadillo m,
  sandwich m
sanitary pads
  compresa higiénica
Saturday sábado m
sauce salsa f
saucer platillo m
sausage salchicha f
save ahorrar
savoury salado/a
say decir
scales balanza f
scarf bufanda f
scenery paisaje m
school escuela f
scissors tijeras fpl
Scot, Scottish (n, adj)
  escocés/escocesa m/f
Scotland Escocia
scrambled eggs
  huevos revueltos
scratch (n) arañazo m

scratch (vb) rascar
screen pantalla f
screw tornillo m
screwdriver
  destornillador m
scrubbing brush
  cepillo para fregar
scuba diving
  submarinismo m
sea mar m/f
seagull gaviota f
seasick mareado/a
seaside costa f
season temporada f
season ticket abono m,
  billete de temporada
seasoning
  condimento m
seat asiento m
seatbelt cinturón de
  seguridad
seaweed alga f
secluded aislado/a
second segundo/a
second-class
  segunda clase
second-hand
  segunda mano
secretary
  secretario/a m/f
security guard
  guardia de seguridad
see ver
self-catering
  alojamiento con cocina
self-employed trabajar
  por cuenta propia

ENGLISH → SPANISH

self-service autoservicio m
sell vender
sell-by date fecha de vencimiento
send enviar
senior citizen jubilado/a m/f
sentence (grammar) frase f
sentence (law) sentencia f
separate separado/a
September septiembre m
septic séptico/a
septic tank tanque séptico
serious serio/a
service servicio m
service charge propina f
serviette servilleta f
set menu menú fijo
several varios/as
sew coser
sex sexo m
shade sombra f
shake agitar
shallow poco profundo
shame vergüenza f
shampoo and set lavar y marcar
share compartir
sharp afilado/a
shave afeitarse
she ella
sheep oveja f

sheet sábana f
shelf estante m
shellfish mariscos mpl
sheltered abrigado/a
shine brillo m
shingle tablilla f
shingles herpes m
ship barco m
shirt camisa f
shock absorber amortiguador m
shoe zapato m
shoelace cordón m
shop tienda f
shop assistant dependiente/a m/f
shop window vitrina f, vidriera f
shopping centre centro comercial
shore costa, orilla f
short corto/a
short-cut atajo m
short-sighted miope
shorts pantalones cortos
should deber
shoulder hombro m
shout (n) grito m
shout (vb) gritar
show (n) espectáculo m
show (vb) mostrar
shower ducha f
shrimp camarón m
shrink encoger
shut cerrar
shutter contraventana f
shy tímido/a

sick, I'm going to be sick! enfermo/a, ¡Voy a vomitar!
side lado m
side dish acompañamiento m
sidewalk acera f, vereda f
sieve colador m
sight vista f
sightseeing turismo m
sign (n) anuncio m
sign (vb) firmar
signal señal f
signature firma f
signpost poste indicador
silence silencio m
silk seda f
silly tonto/a
silver plata f
similar como, parecido/a
simple sencillo/a
sing cantar
singer cantante m/f
single solo, soltero/a
single bed cama de una plaza
single room habitación para uno/single
single ticket billete de ida
sink fregadero m
sister hermana f
sister-in-law cuñada f
sit sentarse
size tamaño, número m
skate (n) patín m

skate (vb) patinar
skating rink pista de patinaje
ski (n) esquí m
ski (vb) esquiar
ski boot bota para esquí
ski jump salto de esquí
ski slope pista para esquiar
skin piel f
skirt falda f
sky cielo m
sledge trineo m
sleep dormir
sleeper, sleeping car coche dormitorio
sleeping bag saco de dormir
sleeping pill pastilla para dormir, somnífero m
sleepy con sueño
slice rebanada f
slide (n, photo) diapositiva f
slide (vb) deslizarse
slip resbalarse
slippers zapatillas fpl
slippery resbaladizo/a
Slovak eslovaco
Slovak Republic República de Eslovaquia
slow lento/a
slowly despacio
small pequeño/a, chico/a
smell oler
smile (vb) sonreír
smoke (n) humo m

ENGLISH → SPANISH

smoke (vb) fumar
smoked salmon salmón ahumado
snack tentempie m, bocadillo m
snake serpiente f
sneeze estornudar
snore roncar
snorkel tubo de respiración
snow, it is snowing nieve, está nevando
soaking solution liquído para remojar
soap jabón m
soap powder jabón en polvo
sober sobrio/a
socket (elec) enchufe m
socks calcetines mpl, medias fpl
soda soda f
soft blando/a, suave
soft drink refesco m, bebida f
sole (fish) lenguado m
sole (shoe) suela f
soluble soluble
some unos/as, algunos/as
someone, somebody alguien, alguna persona
something algo
sometimes a veces
somewhere en algún lugar
son hijo m

son-in-law yerno m
song canción f
soon pronto
sore dolorido/a
sore, it's sore duele, tengo dolor
sore throat dolor de garganta
Sorry! ¡Lo siento! ¡Disculpa!
sort tipo m
soup sopa f
sour agrio/a
south sur m
South Africa Sudáfrica
South African (adj, n) sudafricano/a m/f
souvenir recuerdo m
spade pala f
Spain España
Spaniard, Spanish español/a m/f
spanner llave f, llave de tuercas
spare part parte de repuesto
spare tyre neumático de repuesto
spark plug bujía f
sparkling con gas
speak hablar
speciality especialidad f
spectacles lentes m/f, gafas fpl, anteojos mpl
speed velocidad f
speed limit límite de velocidad

speedometer velocímetro **m**
spell deletrear
spend (money) gastar
spend (time) pasar
spice especia **f**
spider araña **f**
spill derramar
spin-dryer secadora **f**
spinach espinacas **fpl**
spine espinazo **m**
spirit (soul) espíritu **m**
spirits (drink) licores **mpl**
splinter astilla **f**
spoil arruinar
spoke (of wheel) rayo **m**
sponge esponja **f**
sponge cake bizcocho **m**
spoon cuchara **f**
sprain (n) torcedura **f**
sprain (vb) torcer
spring (season) primavera **f**
square cuadro **m**, plaza **f**
stadium estadio **m**
stain mancha **f**
stairs escalera **f**
stale rancio/a
stall puesto **m**
stamp sello **m**, estampilla **f**
staple (n, food) alimento básico
staple (vb) grapar
star estrella **f**

start comenzar, empezar
starter (car) arranque
station estación **f**
stationer's papelería **f**
stationery artículos de escritorio
statue estatua **f**
stay quedarse, parar
steal robar
steam vapor **m**
steep empinado/a
steer dirigir
steering wheel volante **m**
step escalón **m**
stepfather padrastro **m**
stepmother madrastra **f**
stew guiso **m**
stick (vb) pegar
sticking plaster esparadrapo **m**
still (yet) todavía
still (quiet) quieto
sting (n) picadura **f**
sting (vb) picar
stitch puntada **f**
stock (soup) caldo **m**
stocking media **f**
stolen robado
stomach estómago **m**
stomachache dolor de estómago
stone piedra **f**
stop parar
stop sign pare
stopover parada **f**
store (n) tienda **f**

store (vb) almacenar
storey piso m, planta f
storm tormenta f
straight derecho/a
straight on siga derecho
straightaway
directamente
strange raro/a
**strange, stranger
(adj, n)** extraño/a m/f
strap correa f
straw paja f
strawberry fresa f,
frutilla f
stream arroyo m
street calle f
street map
mapa de calles
strike (n) huelga f
string cordel m
striped rayado/a
stroke (n) apoplegía f
strong fuerte
stuck pegado
student estudiante m/f
student discount
descuento de estudiante
stuffed lleno/a, relleno/a
stupid estúpido/a
subtitle subtítulo m
suburb barrio m
subway metro m
suddenly de repente
suede gamuza f
sugar azúcar m/f
sugar-free
no contiene azúcar
suit traje m

suitcase maleta f
summer verano m
summit cumbre f
sun sol m
sunblock crema
para el sol
sunburn quemadura
de sol
Sunday domingo m
sunglasses gafas
de sol
sunny soleado/a
sunrise amanecer m
sunroof techo corredizo
sunset atardecer m
sunshade sombrilla f
sunshine luz del sol
sunstroke insolación f
suntan bronceado m
suntan lotion crema
bronceadora
supper cena f
supplement
suplemento m
sure seguro/a
surfboard
tabla de surfear
**surgery (doctor's
rooms)** consultorio m
surgery (procedure)
cirujía f
surname apellido m
surrounded rodeado
suspension suspensión f
swallow (vb) tragar
swear (an oath) jurar
swear (curse) decir
palabrotas

swear word palabrota f
sweat (n) transpiración f
sweat (vb) sudar
sweater suéter m
Sweden Suecia
Swedish, Swede (adj, n) sueco/a m/f
sweet (adj) dulce
swell hincharse
swelling hinchazón f
swim nadar
swimming costume traje de baño/bañador
swing balanceo m
Swiss (adj, n) suizo/a m/f
Swiss-German suizo-alemán
switch interruptor m
switch off apagar
switch on encender
Switzerland Suiza
swollen hinchado/a
synagogue sinagoga f

T
table mesa f
table wine vino de mesa
tablecloth mantel m
tablespoon cucharón m
tailor sastre m
take tomar
take-away food comida para llevar
talcum powder talco m
talk hablar
tall alto/a
tampon tampón m

tangerine clementina f
tank tanque m
tape cinta f
tape measure cinta para medir
tape recorder grabadora f
taste (n) gusto m
tax impuesto m
taxi taxi m
taxi driver conductor/a de taxi, taxista m/f
taxi rank parada de taxis
tea té m
tea bag bolsa de té
teach enseñar
teacher maestro/a, profesor/a m/f
team equipo m
teapot tetera f
tear (n) desgarrón m
tear (vb) desgarrar
teaspoon cucharilla f
teat (bottle) tetina f
teeth dentadura f
telephone teléfono m
telephone call llamada telefónica
telephone directory directorio telefónico, guía telefónica
television televisión f
tell decir
temperature temperatura f
temple templo m
temporary temporario

ENGLISH → SPANISH

ENGLISH → SPANISH

tendon tendón m
tennis tenis m
tennis court cancha de tenis, pista de tennis
tennis racket raqueta de tenis
tent carpa f
tent peg estaca f
terminal terminal m
thank agradecer
that ese/esa m/f
the el/la/los/las
theatre teatro m
theft robo m
there allí/allá
thermometer termómetro m
they ellos/ellas
thick grueso/a
thief ladrón/ladrona m/f
thigh muslo m
thin flaco/a, delgado/a
thing cosa f
think pensar
third-party insurance seguro contra terceros
thirsty tener sed
this este/esta
this morning esta mañana
this way por aquí
this week esta semana
thorn espina f
those esos/esas
thousand mil m
thread hilado m
throat garganta f

throat lozenges pastillas/caramelos para la garganta
through a través de, por
throw echar
thumb pulgar m
thunder trueno m
thunderstorm tormenta f
Thursday jueves m
ticket billete m, boleto m
ticket collector revisor/a m/f
ticket office despacho de billetes
tide, low tide, high tide marea f, marea baja, marea alta
tie corbata f
tight apretado/a, tirante
tights medias fpl
till (cash register) caja f
till (until) hasta
time hora f
timetable horario m
tin lata f
tin opener abridor de latas
tinfoil papel metálico
tiny minúsculo/a
tip propina f
tired cansado/a
tissue tisú m
to a
toad sapo m
today hoy m

toe dedo del pie

together juntos/as

toilet baño m, servicios **mpl**

tolerate aguantar

toll, toll road peaje m, camino de peaje

tomato tomate m

tomato juice jugo de tomate

tomorrow mañana m

tomorrow morning/ afternoon/evening mañana por la mañana/ tarde/noche

tongue lengua f

tonight esta noche

tonsillitis amigdalitis f

too también

too much demasiado

tool herramienta f

toolkit caja de herramientas

tooth diente m

toothache dolor de muelas

toothbrush cepillo de dientes

toothpick escarbadientes

top parte de arriba

top floor el piso más alto

topless sin camiseta

torch linterna f

torn rasgado

total total m

tough duro/a, fuerte

tour viaje m

tour guide guía de turismo

tour operator operador de turismo

tow remolcar

towel toalla f

tower torre f

town ciudad f

town hall sala municipal, ayuntamiento m

toy juguete m

tracksuit chándal m

traffic tráfico m

traffic jam atascamiento m, embotellamiento m

traffic light semáforo m

trailer remolque m

train tren m

tram tranvía m

tranquillizer droga tranquilizante

translate traducir

translation traducción f

translator traductor/a m/f

trash basura f

travel viajar

travel agent agente de viajes

travel documents documentos de viajes

travel sickness mareo m

traveller's cheque cheque de viaje

tray bandeja f

ENGLISH → SPANISH

tree árbol m
trolley carro m
trouble problemas mpl
trousers pantalones mpl
trout trucha f
truck camión m
true verdadero/a
trunk (of car) baúl,
    maletero m
try intentar
try on probarse
tube tubo m
tuna atún m
tunnel subterráneo m,
    túnel m
turkey pavo m
Turkey Turquía
Turkish, Turk (adj, n)
    turco/a m/f
turn volver
turn around darse vuelta
turn off apagar
turquoise turquesa f
tweezers pinzas fpl
twice dos veces
twin beds camas
    gemelas
twins gemelos
type tipo m
typical típico/a
tyre neumático m
tyre pressure presión
    en los neumáticos

U
ugly feo/a
ulcer úlcera f
umbrella paraguas m

uncle tío m
uncomfortable
    incómodo/a
unconscious
    inconciente
under bajo
underdone poco hecho
underground (adj)
    subterráneo/a
**underground
    (n, subway)** metro m
underpants ropa interior
understand
    comprender, entender
underwear ropa interior
unemployed
    desempleado/a
United Kingdom Reino
    Unido
United States
    Estados Unidos
university universidad f
unleaded petrol
    combustible sin plomo
unlimited ilimitado/a
unlock abrir
unpack desembalar
unscrew destornillar
until hasta
unusual insólito/a
up arriba
up-market superior
upside down al revés
upstairs al piso de arriba
urgent urgente
us nos, nosotros/as
use usar
useful útil

usual corriente
usually generalmente

V
vacancy habitación libre
vacation vacaciones fpl
vaccine vacuna f
vacuum cleaner
  aspiradora f
valid válido/a
valley valle m
valuable de valor
value valor m
valve válvula f
van camioneta f
VAT Impuesto sobre
  Valor Añadido (IVA)
veal ternera f
vegetables
  verduras fpl,
  vegetales mpl
vegetarian
  vegetariano/a m/f
vehicle vehículo m
vein vena f
vending machine
  máquina expendedora
venereal disease
  enfermedad de
  trasmisión sexual
very muy
very well pura vida
vest camisetilla f
vet (veterinarian)
  veterinario/a m/f
via vía, por
Vienna Viena
view vista f

village pueblo m
vinegar vinagre m
vineyard viñedo m
violet (adj, n) violeta f
virus virus m
visa visa f
visit visitar
visiting hours
  horario de visita
visitor visitante m/f
voice voz f
volcano volcán m
voltage voltaje m
vomit vomitar
voucher vale m,
  cupón m

W
wage salario, sueldo m
waist cintura f
waistcoat chaleco m
wait esperar
waiter/waitress
  camarero/a, mozo/a m/f
waiting room
  sala de espera
wake up despertar
wake-up call
  llamada para despertar
Wales Gales
walk caminar, andar
wall muro m, pared f
wallet billetera f
walnut nuez f
want querer
war guerra f
ward (hospital) sala f

ENGLISH → SPANISH

wardrobe guardarropa **m**
warehouse almacén **m**
warm cálido/a
wash lavar
washbasin lavabo **m**
washing powder polvo de lavar
washing-up liquid líquido para lavar, detergente **m**
wasp avispa **f**
waste residuo **m**
waste bin bote de residuos/bote de basura
watch (n) reloj **m**
watch (vb) mirar
watch strap correa de reloj
water agua **f**
watermelon sandía **f**
waterproof a prueba de agua
water-skiing esquí acuático
wave ola **f**
we nosotros/as
weak débil
wear llevar, usar
weather tiempo **m**
weather forecast pronóstico del tiempo
web red **f**
wedding boda **f**
wedding present regalo de boda
wedding ring anillo de boda

Wednesday miércoles **m**
week - last week, this week, next week, a week ago semana **f** – semana pasada, esta semana, semana próxima, hace una semana
weekday día de semana
weekend fin de semana
weekly semanalmente
weigh pesar
weight peso **m**
weird raro/a
welcome bienvenido/a
well bien
Welsh, Welshman, Welshwoman (adj, n) galés/galesa **m/f**
were era/estaba
west oeste **m**
wet mojado/a
wetsuit traje de agua
What? ¿Qué?
What is wrong? ¿Hay algo mal/malo?
What's the matter? ¿Qué pasa?
What's the time? ¿Qué hora es?
wheel rueda **f**
wheel clamp cepo **m**
wheelchair silla de rueda
When? ¿Cuándo?
Where? ¿Dónde?
Which? ¿Cuál?
while mientras

whipped cream nata montada
white blanco/a
Who? ¿Quién?
whole (adj) entero/a
whole (n) todo m
wholemeal bread pan integral de trigo
Whose? ¿De quién?
Why? ¿Por qué?
wide ancho/a
widower, widow viudo/a m/f
wife esposa f
wig peluca f
win ganar
wind viento m
window ventana f
window seat asiento en ventanilla
windscreen parabrisas m
windscreen wiper limpiaparabrisas m
windy ventoso/a
wine vino m
wine glass copa f
winter invierno m
wire cable m
wish desear
with con
without sin
witness testigo m/f
wolf lobo m
woman mujer f
wood madera f
wool lana f
word palabra f

work trabajar
world mundo m
worried preocupado/a
worse peor
worth de valor
wrap up envolver
wrapping paper papel de envolver
wrinkles arrugas fpl
wrist muñeca f
write escribir
writing paper papel de escribir

X
X-ray radiografía f

Y
yacht yate m
year año m
yellow amarillo/a
yellow pages páginas amarillas
yes sí
yesterday ayer m
yolk yema f
you tú
young jóven
your tu
youth hostel albergue juvenil

Z
zero cero m
zipper, zip fastener cremallera f
zone zona f
zoo jardín zoológico

ENGLISH → SPANISH

SPANISH → ENGLISH

A

a to
a él to him
a la parrilla grilled
a pesar de although
a prueba de agua
waterproof
a puertas adentro
indoors
a través de through
a veces sometimes
abadía f abbey
abajo downstairs
abeja f bee
abierto/a open
abogado/a m/f lawyer
abono m season ticket
aborto m abortion
abridor de botellas
bottle opener
abridor de latas can
opener, tin opener
abrigado/a sheltered
abrigo m coat, jacket,
overcoat
abrigo de piel fur coat
abrir unlock
abrochar fasten
absceso m abscess
abuelo/a m/f grand-
father, grandmother
abuelos mpl
grandparents
aburrido boring
acá here, over here
acampar camp (vb)
acantilado m cliff
accidente m accident

accidente de tráfico
road accident
acedía f heartburn
aceite m oil
aceite de oliva olive oil
aceituna f olive
acelerador m
accelerator
acento m accent
aceptar accept
acera f sidewalk
acompañamiento m
side dish
aconsejar advise
acostarse lie down
acuerdo m agreement
adaptador m adapter
adelantar overtake
adentro inside
adiós goodbye
aduana f customs
adulto/a m/f adult
(adj, n)
aeropuerto m airport
afeitarse shave
afilado/a sharp
afuera out, outside
afueras countryside,
outskirts
agarrar catch
agenda f diary
agente de policía
policeman/woman
agente de viajes
travel agent
agente inmobilario/a
estate agent
agitar shake

agotado/a exhausted
agradable nice
agradecer thank
agradecido/a grateful
agrio/a sour
agua f water
agua mineral mineral water
agua potable drinking water
aguamala f jellyfish
aguantar put up with, tolerate
águila f eagle
aguja f needle
aguja de tejer knitting needle
aguja hipodérmica hypodermic needle
agujero m hole, leak
ahora now
ahorrar save
aire m air
aire acondicionado air conditioning
aislado/a secluded
ajedrez m chess
ajo m garlic
ajustar fasten
ajustar el cinturón de seguridad fasten seatbelt
al aire libre outdoors
al fondo at the bottom
al piso de arriba upstairs
al principio at first
al revés upside down

aladeltismo hang-gliding
alambrada f fence
alba f dawn (n)
albergue m hostel
albergue juvenil youth hostel
alegría f joy
alemán, alemana m/f German (adj, n)
Alemania Germany
aletas fpl flippers
alfiler m pin
alfombra f carpet, rug
alga f seaweed
algo something
algodón m cotton
algodón hidrófilo cotton wool
alguien someone, somebody
alguna persona someone, somebody
algunos/as some
alicates mpl pliers
alimentar feed (vb)
alimento m food
alimento básico staple (food)
aliño m salad dressing
allá over there
allí/allá there
almacén m food shop, warehouse
almacenar store (vb)
almendra f almond
almohada f pillow
almohadón m cushion

SPANISH → ENGLISH

almuerzo m lunch
alojamiento m accommodation
alojamiento con cocina self-catering
alquilar let, hire, rent (vb)
alquiler m rent (n)
alquiler de coches car hire
alto/a high, tall
altura f height
amable kind
amanecer m sunrise, dawn
amapola f poppy
amar love (vb)
amarillo/a yellow
amarradero m mooring
ámbar m amber
ambos both
ambulancia f ambulance
amigable friendly
amigdalitis f tonsillitis
amigo/a m/f friend
amigo/a invisible penfriend
amigo/a por carta penfriend
amor m love (n)
amortiguador m shock absorber
ampliación f enlargement
ampolla f blister
amueblado furnished

analgésico m painkiller
ananá m pineapple
ancho/a wide
andar go, walk
andar conducir drive, go by car
andar en bicicleta cycle (vb)
andar manejar drive, go by car
andén m platform
anestésico m anaesthetic
angosto/a narrow
anguila f eel
anillo m ring (n)
anillo de boda wedding ring
animal m animal
animal doméstico pet
aniversario m anniversary
anoche last night
año m year
Año Nuevo New Year
anteojos mpl spectacles, glasses
antes before
antiácido antacid
anticonceptivo m/f contraceptive
antiparras fpl goggles
anual annual
anuncio m sign (n)
apagado/a dull, gloomy
apagar switch off, turn off
aparcar park (vb)

apartamento m apartment, flat
apellido m surname
apenas hardly
apendicitis f appendicitis
apio m celery
aplazar postpone
apoplegía f stroke (n)
apostar bet
aprender learn
apretado/a tight
aproximadamente about, approximately, roughly
aquí here, over here
araña f spider
arañazo m scratch (n)
árbol m tree
arbusto m bush
archivo m file (folder)
área f area
arena f sand
arma f gun
armada f navy
armario m cupboard, locker
aros mpl earrings
arranque starter (car)
arreglar arrange, fix
arrendar lease (vb)
arrestar arrest
arriba up
arroyo m stream
arroz m rice
arrugas fpl wrinkles
arruinar spoil
arte m art

artesanía f craft
artículos de escritorio stationery
artista m/f artist
ascensor m lift, elevator
asiento m seat
asiento de coche para niños child car seat
asiento en el pasillo aisle seat
asiento en ventanilla window seat
asociarse join
áspero/a rough
aspiradora f vacuum cleaner
asqueroso/a revolting
astilla f splinter
asunto m matter
asunto escrito printed matter
atacar attack (vb)
atajo m short-cut
ataque m attack (n)
ataque al corazón heart attack
atardecer m sunset
atascamiento m traffic jam
ático m attic
atropellar knock over
atún m tuna
audiencia f audience
audífono m hearing aid
auricular m receiver (telephone)

SPANISH → ENGLISH

auriculares mpl earphones, headphones
auténtico/a genuine
auto m car
autobús m bus
autocar m coach
autopista f freeway, motorway
autoservicio m self-service
avalancha f avalanche
ave f bird
avellana f hazelnut
avena f oats
avenida f avenue
avería f breakdown (car)
avión m aeroplane, plane
aviso m advertisement
avispa f wasp
ayer m yesterday
¡Ayuda! Help!
ayudar help (vb)
ayuntamiento m town hall
azúcar m/f sugar
azul blue
azul marino navy blue

B
bacalao m cod
bache m pothole
bahía f bay
bailar dance (vb)
bajar get off
bajas calorías low fat
bajo below, under

bajo/a low
bajo llave locked in
balanceo m swing
balanza f scales
balcón m balcony
balde m bucket
bandeja f tray
bañera f bath
baño m bathroom, cloakroom, lavatory, toilet
baño de hombres gents' toilet
baño de mujeres ladies' toilet
bar gay gay bar
barato/a cheap
barba f beard
barbería f barber's shop
barbilla f chin
barco m boat, ship
barra f loaf
barra de chocolate bar of chocolate
barranca abajo downhill
barril m barrel
barrio m area, district, suburb
barro m mud
bastante fairly
basura f litter, refuse, rubbish, trash
bata f dressing gown
batería descargada flat battery
baúl m trunk

beber drink (vb)
bebida f drink, soft drink
belga m/f Belgian (adj, n)
Bélgica Belgium
besar kiss (vb)
beso m kiss (n)
biblioteca f library
bicicleta f bicycle
bien OK, well
bienvenido/a welcome
bigote m moustache
billete m ticket
billete abierto open
   ticket
billete aéreo air ticket
billete de ida single
   ticket
billete de ida y vuelta
   return ticket
billete de temporada
   season ticket
billetera f wallet
binoculares binoculars
bizcocho m sponge
   cake
blanco/a white
blando/a soft
blanquear bleach (vb)
bloqueado blocked
bloqueo automático
   central locking
blusa f blouse
boca f mouth
bocadillo m sandwich,
   snack
bocina f horn (car)
boda f wedding
bodega f cellar

boleto m ticket
**boleto de estaciona-
   miento** parking ticket
boli m pen
bolígrafo m ballpoint
   pen
bolsa f bag, carrier bag
**bolsa de agua
   caliente** hot-water
   bottle
bolsa de plástico
   plastic bag
bolsillo m pocket
bolsita de té tea bag
bolso m handbag,
   purse
bomberos mpl fire
   brigade
bombilla f light bulb
bombones mpl
   chocolates
bonito/a beautiful, pretty
borde m border, edge
borracho/a m/f
   drunk (adj, n)
bosque m forest
bota para esquí
   ski boot
botas fpl boots
bote m boat, dinghy
**bote de residuos/
   basura** waste bin
botella f bottle
botón m button
bragas fpl knickers,
   panties
brandy m brandy
brillante bright

SPANISH → ENGLISH

brillo m shine
brisa f breeze
broche m brooch
broches para la ropa
  clothes peg
broma f joke
bronceado m suntan
bronquitis f bronchitis
Bruselas Brussels
bucear dive
buena suerte
  good luck
buenas noches
  good night
buenas tardes
  good afternoon,
  good evening
bueno/a good
buenos días good
  morning, good day
bufanda f scarf
bujía f spark plug
bulbo m bulb (plant)
buscar fetch, look for
buzón m letterbox,
  postbox

C

caballo m horse
cabello m hair
cabeza f head
cabina f cabin
cabina telefónica
  phone booth
cable m wire
cable de extensión
  extension lead

cables de conexion
  de batería
  jump leads
cabra f goat
cacahuete m peanut
cacao m cocoa
cacerola f pan
cada each, every
cada hora hourly (adj)
cada uno everyone
cadera f hip
caducar expire
caer fall
café m coffee
café helado m
  iced coffee
café instantáneo
  instant coffee
caja f box, carton, cash
  desk, cash register, till
caja de cambios
  gearbox
caja de fusibles
  fuse box
caja de herramientas
  toolkit
caja fuerte safe (n)
cajero/a m/f cashier
cajero automático
  auto-teller,
  cash dispenser
cajón m drawer
calambre m cramp
calcetines mpl socks
calculadora f calculator
caldo m stock
calefacción f heating

calefacción central central heating

calefactor m heater

calidad f quality

cálido/a warm

caliente hot

calle f road, street

calle de una sola mano one-way street

calle principal/mayor main road

calma calm

calor m heat

calzada f pavement

cama f bed

cama de una plaza single bed

cama doble double bed

cámara de aire inner tube

camarera f chambermaid

camarero/a m/f waiter, waitress

camarón m shrimp

camas gemelas twin beds

cambiador m fitting room

cambiar change (vb)

cambio m change, exchange (n)

caminar walk

camino m road

camino circular ring road

camino de peaje toll road

camión m truck

camión de reparación de averías breakdown van

camioneta f lorry, van

camisa f shirt

camisetilla f vest

campamento m campsite

campamento de remolques caravan site

campana f bell

campo m countryside, field

campo de golf golf course

Canadá Canada

canal m canal, channel

Canal de la Mancha English Channel

canasta f basket

cancelación f cancellation

cancelar cancel

cáncer m cancer

cancha de tenis tennis court

canción f song

candado m padlock

cangrejo m crab

canoa f canoe

cansado/a tired

cantante m/f singer

cantar sing

cantidad f amount, quantity

caña de pescar fishing rod

cañería f pipe (plumbing)

capilla f chapel

capital f capital (city)

capital m capital (money)

capó/capota m/f bonnet, hood (car)

capucha f hood (garment)

cara f face

caramelos para la garganta throat lozenges

carbón m charcoal, coal

carburador m carburettor

cárcel f prison

cargar carry, charge

carnada f bait

carne f meat

carne de puerco/ cerdo pork

carne de vaca f beef

carne medio hecha medium rare (meat)

carne picada minced meat

carné m card

carné de identidad identity card

carnet de conducir driving licence

carnicero/a m/f butcher

caro/a expensive

carpa f tent

carpeta f file (folder)

carpintero/a m/f carpenter

carrera f race (sport)

carrera de caballos horse racing

carretera f road

carretera de circunvalación bypass (road)

carretera en obras road works

carril m lane

carrito para equipaje luggage trolley

carro m car, trolley

carta f card, letter

carta de vinos wine list

cartera f handbag

carterista f pickpocket

cartero/a m/f postman/postwoman

cartón m cardboard

casa f home, house

casado/a married

casco m helmet, crash helmet

casi almost, nearly

casilla de correo post office box

caso m case

cassette f cassette

castaño m chestnut

castillo m castle

catedral f cathedral
católico/a m/f
  Catholic (adj, n)
caucho m rubber
cazar hunt
cebo m bait
cebolla f onion
cebolleta f chives
celoso/a jealous
cementerio m
  cemetery
cena f dinner, supper
centígrado Centigrade
centímetro m
  centimetre
centro m centre
centro comercial
  shopping centre
centro de la ciudad
  city centre
centro musical
  CD player
cepillo m brush (n)
cepillo de dientes
  toothbrush
cepillo de pelo
  hairbrush
cepillo de uñas
  nailbrush
cepillo para fregar
  scrubbing brush
cepo m wheel clamp
cera f polish (n)
cerámica f pottery
cerca near, nearby (adv)
cercano/a near,
  nearby (adj)
cerdo m pig

cereza f cherry
cero m zero
cerrado/a closed,
  blocked
cerradura f lock (n)
cerrar lock, lock out,
  shut
certeza certain
certificado m
  certificate
**certificado de
  nacimiento**
  birth certificate
certificar register (vb)
cerveza f beer
**cerveza de barril/
  tirada** draught beer
cerveza rubia lager
césped m grass
cesta f basket
chaleco m waistcoat,
  pullover
chaleco salvavidas
  life jacket
champán m
  champagne
champiñon m
  mushroom
chancletas fpl
  flip-flops
chándal m tracksuit
chaqueta f jacket
chaval/a m/f child
cheque m cheque
cheque de viaje
  traveller's cheque
chícharo m pea
chicle m chewing gum

chico/a small
chico/a m/f child
chimenea f chimney
China China
chocar crash (vb)
chocolate m chocolate
chófer m driver
chupete m dummy, pacifier
chupón lollipop
ciego/a blind (adj)
cielo m sky
cielo raso ceiling
ciertamente certainly
cigarrillo m cigarette
cine m cinema
cinta f ribbon, tape
cinta adhesiva f adhesive tape
cinta para medir tape measure
cintura f waist
cinturón m belt
cinturón de seguridad safety belt, seatbelt
cinturón salvavidas life belt
círculo m circle
ciruela f plum
cirujía f surgery (procedure)
cisterna f cistern
cistitis f cystitis
cita f appointment, date
ciudad f city, town
ciudadano/a m/f citizen

claro absolutely, certainly
claro/a clear, light (adj, colour)
clase f class, lesson
clase económica economy class
clavícula f collarbone
clavija f peg
clementina f tangerine
cliente m/f client, customer
clima m climate
clínica f clinic
club de golf golf club (place)
cobertor quilt, bedspread
cobrar excesiva- mente overcharge
Coca Cola f Coke
coche m car
coche comedor buffet car
coche de alquiler hire car
coche dormitorio sleeper, sleeping car
cochecito m pram
cochecito de niño buggy
cocina f cooker, kitchen
cocinar cook (vb)
cocinero/a m/f cook (n), chef
cocinilla f kitchenette
coco m coconut
código m code

código postal postal code

codo m elbow

coger catch

cola f queue (n)

colador m colander, sieve

colchón f mattress

colega m/f colleague

colgar hang up (telephone)

coliflor f cauliflower

collar m necklace

color m colour

colorear dye (vb)

colorete m blusher

combustible m gas, fuel, petrol

combustible sin plomo unleaded petrol

comedia f comedy

comedor m dining room

comenzar start

comer eat

comida f food, meal

comida de campo picnic

comida envenenada food poisoning

comida para bebé baby food

comida para llevar take-away food

comisaría f police station

como like, similar to

¿Cómo? How?

¿Cómo estás? How do you do? How are you?

cómoda f chest of drawers

cómodo/a comfortable

compañero/a m/f partner (companion)

compañía f company

compartimento m compartment

compartir share

compás m compass

complejo turístico resort

completamente completely, quite

compositor/a m/f composer

comprar buy

comprender understand

compresa higiénica sanitary pads

comprometido/a engaged (to be married)

computadora f computer

Comunidad Europea EC

con with

con experiencia experienced

con fluidez fluent

con frecuencia often

con gas fizzy, sparkling

con hambre hungry

SPANISH → ENGLISH

con sueño sleepy
concesión f
  concession
conciente conscious
concierto m concert
condición f condition
condimento m
  seasoning
**condimento para
  ensalada** salad
  dressing
condón m condom
**conducción a la
  derecha**
  right-hand drive
**conducción a la
  izquierda**
  left-hand drive
conducir drive
conductor/a m/f driver
conductor/a de taxi
  taxi driver
conejo/a m/f rabbit
conexión f connection
  (elec)
conferencia f
  conference
confirmación f
  confirmation
confirmar confirm
confundido/a confused
confundir mix up (vb)
confusión f mix-up (n)
congelado/a frozen
congelador m freezer
conmoción cerebral
  concussion
conocer know

consejo m advice
construir build
consulado m consulate
consultorio m surgery
  (doctor's rooms)
contacto m contact (n)
contador m meter
contaminado polluted
**contenedor de
  gasolina** petrol can
contestar reply (vb)
continuar continue
contra against
contrato m contract
contrato de alquiler
  lease (n)
contraventana f
  shutter
control de pasaporte
  pass control
contundente blunt
conveniente
  convenient
copa f wine glass
copiar copy
corazón m heart
corbata f tie
corcho m cork
cordel m string
cordero m lamb,
  mutton
cordón m shoelace
coro m choir
corona f crown
correa f strap
correa de reloj
  watch strap

correa del ventilador
fanbelt
correctamente
properly
correcto/a correct (adj)
correo m mail, post (n)
correo aéreo airmail
correo central main
post office
correo certificado
registered mail
correr run, jog (vb)
corriente usual
corriente f current (n),
draught
cortar chop, cut
corte de electricidad
power cut
corte de pelo haircut
cortijo m farmhouse
cortina f curtain
corto/a short
cosa f thing
cosecha f harvest
coser sew
costa f coast, seaside
coste, costo m cost
costilla f rib
costumbre f custom
creer believe
crema f cream
crema bronceadora
suntan lotion
crema hidratante
moisturizer
crema limpiadora
cleansing lotion

crema para el sol
sunblock
crema pastelera
custard
cremallera f zipper,
zip fastener
crepe f pancake
criada f maid
cristal m crystal
cruce m crossing,
junction, intersection
cruce a nivel level
crossing
cruce de caminos
crossroads
crucero m cruise (n)
crucigrama m
crossword puzzle
crudo/a raw
cruz m cross (n)
cruzar cross (vb)
cuaderno m notebook
cuadro m painting,
square
¿Cuál? Which?
cualquier cosa
anything
cualquiera anybody
¿Cuándo? When?
¿Cuánto/a? How
many?
¿Cuánto es? How
much is it?
cuarentena f
quarantine
cuarto m quarter, room
cuatro por cuatro
four-wheel drive

SPANISH → ENGLISH

cubertería f cutlery
cubo m bucket, pail
cubo de la basura
  bin, dustbin
cucaracha f cockroach
cuchara f spoon
cucharilla f teaspoon
cucharón m
  tablespoon
cuchillo m knife
cuello m collar, neck
cuenco m bowl
cuenta f account, bill
cuerda f rope
cuerno m horn (animal)
cuero m leather
cuerpo m body
cuesta abajo downhill
cuestión f question
cueva f cave
cuidado careful
cuidar look after
culpa f fault
cumbre f summit
cumpleaños m
  birthday
cuna f cot
cuna portable
  carry-cot
cuñada f sister-in-law
cuñado m
  brother-in-law
cupón m voucher
cura m priest
curso m course
curso de idioma
  language course

D
dados mpl dice
daltónico/a
  colour-blind
dama f lady
daño m damage
dar give
dar marcha atrás
  reverse (vb)
darse cuenta realize
darse prisa rush,
  hurry (vb)
darse vuelta roll, turn
  around
dátil m date (fruit)
datos mpl details
de from (origin), of
de moda fashionable
de otra forma
  otherwise (differently)
¿De quién? Whose?
de repente suddenly
de valor valuable,
  worth
de vez en cuando
  occasionally
deber must, have to,
  owe, should
débil weak
decepcionado/a
  disappointed
decidir decide
decir say, tell
decir palabrotas
  swear (curse)
decisión f decision
dedo m finger
dedo del pie toe

defecto m fault
defectuoso/a faulty
definitivamente
definitely
dejar leave, let, allow
dejar encerrado
lock out
delantal m apron
deletrear spell
delgado/a thin
deliberadamente
deliberately
delicioso/a delicious
delito m crime
demasiado plenty,
too much
demora f delay (n)
dentadura f teeth
dentaduras dentures
dentista m/f dentist
dentro among, inside
dependiente/a m/f
shop assistant
depósito m deposit
derecho/a right,
straight
derramar spill
derretir melt
derribar knock down
derrumbarse
collapse (vb)
desagüe m drain (n)
desaparecer
disappear
desaparecido/a
missing
desarrollar develop
desastre m disaster

desayuno m breakfast
descafeinado/a
decaffeinated
descansar rest (relax)
desconectado
disconnected
descontar deduct
describir describe
descripción f
description
descubrir discover
descuento m discount
**descuento de
estudiante**
student discount
desde from (time)
desear wish
desembalar unpack
desempleado/a
unemployed
desfiladero m pass (n)
desgarrar tear (vb)
desgarrón m tear (n)
desierto m desert
desinfectante m
disinfectant
desinfectante bucal
mouthwash
deslizarse slide (vb)
**desmaquillador para
ojos** eye make-up
remover
desmayarse faint (vb)
despacho de billetes
ticket office
despacio slowly
desperfecto m flaw

despertar awake, wake up

desprendimiento de tierras landslide

después after, afterwards

destino m destination

destornillador m screwdriver

destornillar unscrew

desviación bypass

desvío m detour

detalles mpl details

detergente m cleaning solution, detergent, washing-up liquid

detrás behind

deudas fpl debts

devolver give back, refund (vb)

día m day

día de semana weekday

día feriado public holiday

diabético/a m/f diabetic (adj, n)

diamante m diamond

diapositiva f slide (photo)

diariamente daily

diario m diary

diarrea f diarrhoea

dibujo m drawing

diccionario m dictionary

diciembre m December

diente m tooth

diesel m diesel

dieta f diet

diferencia f difference

diferente different

difícil difficult

Dinamarca Denmark

dínamo f dynamo

dinero m money

dinero efectivo cash

Dios m God

dirección f direction

directamente straightaway

directo/a direct (adj)

directorio telefónico telephone directory

dirigir steer

disco m disk, record (n, music)

disco de aparcamiento parking disc

disco duro hard disk

¿Disculpa? Pardon?

¡Disculpa! Sorry!

disculpa f apology, excuse (n)

discutir quarrel (vb)

disfrutar enjoy

disponible available

distancia f distance

distrito m district

diversión f fun (n)

divertido/a fun (adj)

divorciado divorced

dobladillo m hem

doblar bend
doble double
docena f dozen
documento m
document, record
(legal)
**documento de
identidad** identity
card
documentos de viajes
travel documents
doler hurt (vb)
dolor m ache, pain
dolor de cabeza
headache
dolor de espalda
backache
dolor de estómago
stomachache
dolor de garganta
sore throat
dolor de muelas
toothache
dolor de oídos
earache
dolorido/a sore
doloroso/a painful
doméstico/a domestic
domingo m Sunday
¿Dónde? Where?
donut m doughnut
dormir sleep
dos veces twice
droga f drug (narcotic)
droga mitigadora
painkiller
droga tranquilizante
tranquillizer

ducha f shower
duele it hurts
dueño/a m/f owner
dulce sweet (adj)
dulce m candy
durante during
durante la noche
overnight
duro/a hard, tough

E
echar throw
echar de menos
homesickness
economía f economy
edad f age
edificio m building
**edificio de aparta-
mentos** block of flats
edredón m duvet, quilt
educado/a formal,
polite
efectivo cash
ejemplo m example
él he, him
él/ella/ello it (subject)
el/los the
el piso más alto
top floor
elástico/a elastic
electricidad f electricity
electricista m/f
electrician
eléctrico/a electric
elegante posh
elegir choose
elevador lift, elevator

SPANISH → ENGLISH

elevador de silla chair lift

ella she

ellos/ellas they

embajada f embassy

embarazada pregnant

embotellamiento m traffic jam

embrague m clutch (car)

emergencia f emergency

empacar pack (vb)

empanada f pie

empaste m filling (tooth)

empezar start

empinado/a steep

empujar push

en at, in, into, on

en algún lugar somewhere

en el extranjero abroad

en forma fit (healthy)

en los alrededores nearby

en lugar de instead

¡Encantado! Pleased to meet you!

encantado/a glad

encendedor m cigarette lighter

encender switch on

encendido m ignition

enchufe m plug, socket (elec)

encoger shrink

encontrar find, meet

enero m January

enfadado angry

enfermedad f disease, illness

enfermedad de trasmisión sexual venereal disease

enfermero/a m/f nurse

enfermo/a ill, sick

¡Enhorabuena! Congratulations!

enojado angry

ensalada f salad

enseñar teach

ensuciar litter (vb)

entender understand

entero/a whole (adj)

entrada f admission fee, cover charge, entrance, entrance fee

entrar enter

entre come in

entrega f delivery

entregar deliver

entusiasmante exciting

enviar send

enviar por correo mail, post (vb)

envolver wrap up

epilepsia f epilepsy

epiléptico/a epileptic

equipaje m baggage, luggage

equipaje de mano hand luggage

equipo m equipment, gear, team
era/estaba were
error m error, mistake
erupción f rash
es/está is
escalera f ladder, stairs
escalera mecánica escalator
escalfado poached
escalón m step
escapar escape (vb)
escarbadientes toothpick
escayola f plaster
escoba f broom
escocés/escocesa m/f Scot, Scottish (n, adj)
Escocia Scotland
escoger choose
esconder hide
escribir write
escritorio m desk
escuchar hear, listen
escuela f school
ese/esa m/f that
esencial essential
eslovaco Slovak
esmalte de uñas nail varnish/polish
esos/esas those
espalda f back
España Spain
español/a m/f Spaniard, Spanish
esparadrapo m sticking plaster

especia f spice
especialidad f speciality
especialmente especially
espectáculo m show (n)
espectáculo de marionetas puppet show
espejo m mirror
espejo retrovisor rear-view mirror
esperanza f hope
esperar expect, wait
esperar con ilusión look forward to
espina f thorn
espinacas fpl spinach
espinazo m spine
espiral f coil (n, contraceptive)
espíritu m spirit
esponja f sponge
esposa f wife
esposo m husband
esquí m ski (n)
esquí acuático water-skiing
esquiar ski (vb)
esquina f corner
está bien all right
esta mañana this morning
esta noche tonight
esta semana this week
estaca f tent peg
estación f station

estación de ferrocarril/tren railway station

estación de policía police station

estación de servicio petrol station

estadio m stadium

Estados Unidos United States

estafa f rip-off

estampilla f stamp, postage stamp

están are

estante m shelf

estar be

estar de acuerdo agree

estatua f statue

este m east

este/esta this

estómago m stomach

Estonia Estonia

estornudar sneeze

estrecho/a narrow

estrella f star

estreñido/a constipated

estudiante m/f student

estufilla f gas cooker

estúpido/a stupid

etiqueta f label, luggage tag

Europa Europe

europeo/a European (adj, n)

evitar avoid

exactamente exactly

exacto accurate

examen m examination

excelente excellent

excepto except

exceso de equipaje excess luggage

excluir exclude

excursión f excursion

experimentado/a experienced

explicar explain

explosión f explosion

explotar burst

exportar export

exposición f exhibition, exposure

expreso m express (train)

extensión f extension

extintor de fuego fire extinguisher

extra extra

extranjero/a m/f foreign, foreigner (adj, n)

extraño/a m/f strange, stranger (adj, n)

extraordinario/a extraordinary

F

fábrica f factory

fábrica de cerveza brewery

fabuloso amazing

fachada f façade

fácil easy

facsímil fax

factura f invoice

falda f skirt
falso/a fake (adj), false
familia f family
famoso/a famous
farmacéutico/a m/f
  chemist, pharmacist
farmacia f pharmacy
faro m headlight
fascinante astonishing
favorito/a favourite
febrero m February
fecha f date (of year)
fecha de nacimiento
  date of birth
fecha de vencimiento
  sell-by date
felicitaciones fpl
  congratulations
feliz happy
¡Feliz Año Nuevo!
  Happy New Year!
¡Feliz Semana Santa!
  Happy Easter!
feo/a ugly, awful
feria f fair (fête)
ferretería f DIY shop,
  hardware shop,
  ironmonger's
ferrocarril m railway
ferry m ferry
festival m festival
fibra sintética
  man-made fibre
fiebre f fever
fiebre del heno
  hay fever
fiesta f party
  (celebration)

fiesta nacional
  public holiday
fila f row (n)
filete m fillet
film a color colour film
filmar film (vb)
filtro m filter
fin de semana
  weekend
final m end
finalmente eventually
fino/a fine (adj)
firma f signature
firmar sign (vb)
flaco/a thin
flor f flower
florista m/f florist
folleto m brochure,
  leaflet
fontanero/a m/f
  plumber
forma f form (shape)
formal formal
formulario m form
  (document)
**formulario de
  inscripción**
  registration form
fósforos mpl
  matches (for lighting)
foto f photo, picture
fotocopia f
  photocopy (n)
fotografía f
  photograph (n)
fotografiar
  photograph (vb)
fractura f fracture

SPANISH → ENGLISH

SPANISH → ENGLISH

frágil breakable
frambuesa f
  raspberry
francés/francesa m/f
  French, Frenchman/
  woman (adj, n)
Francia France
franela f flannel
franqueo m postage
frasco m jar
frase f sentence
  (grammar)
frecuente frequent
fregadero m sink
freír fry
freno m brake (n)
freno de mano
  handbrake
frente f forehead
frente m front
fresa f strawberry
fresco/a cool, fresh
frijol m bean
frío/a cold
frito/a fried
fruta f fruit
frutilla f strawberry
fuego m fire
fuente f fountain
fuera away, out, outside
fuerte strong, tough
fuerte m fortress
fumar smoke (vb)
funda para almohada
  pillowcase
funda para edredón
  duvet cover
funeral m funeral

funicular m funicular
furúnculo m boil (n)
fusible m fuse
fútbol m football
futuro m future

G
gafas fpl glasses,
  spectacles
gafas de sol
  sunglasses
gafas protectoras
  goggles
galería f gallery
Gales Wales
galés/galesa m/f
  Welsh, Welshman,
  Welshwoman (adj, n)
galleta f biscuit, cookie
galón m gallon
gamba f prawn
gamuza f suede
ganar win
ganso m goose
garaje m garage
garantía f guarantee
garganta f throat
gas m gas
gasolina f petrol, fuel
gasolinera f petrol
  station
gastar spend (money)
gastos mpl expenses
gato m jack (car)
gato/a m/f cat
gaviota f seagull
gay gay
gemelos twins

gemelos mpl cufflinks
general general
generalmente mostly, usually
generoso/a generous
gente f folk, people
genuino/a genuine
gerente m/f manager
gimnasio m gym
Ginebra Geneva
giro m money order
glaciar m glacier
gobierno m government
golpear hit, knock
goma f rubber
goma de mascar chewing gum
gordo/a fat
gorro m cap
gota f drop (n)
gotas para los ojos eye drops
gotear leak (vb)
gótico/a Gothic
grabadora f tape recorder
gracioso/a funny
grado degree (measurement)
gradualmente gradually
gramática f grammar
gramo m gram
gran, grande great, big, large
Gran Bretaña Great Britain

grandes almacenes mpl department store
grandioso/a grand
granero m barn
granizo m hail
granja f farm
granjero/a m/f farmer
grapar staple
graso/a fatty, greasy
Grecia Greece
griego/a m/f Greek (adj, n)
gripe f flu
gris grey
gritar shout (vb)
grito m shout (n)
grosella negra blackcurrant
grosella roja redcurrant
grueso/a thick
grupo m group
guantes mpl gloves
guapo/a handsome
guardabarros m bumper, fender
guardar keep
guardar en el armario lock in
guardarropa m wardrobe
¡Guarde el cambio! Keep the change!
guardería de niños crèche
guardería infantil nursery school
guardia m/f guard

SPANISH → ENGLISH

guardia costera
coastguard
guardia de seguridad
security guard
guerra f war
guía m/f guide
guía de turismo guide
book, tour guide
guía telefónica
telephone directory
guisante m pea
guiso m stew
guitarra f guitar
gusano m maggot
gustar like (vb)
gusto m taste

H
haba f bean
habitación f room
habitación doble
double room
habitación libre
vacancy
**habitación para
uno/single** single
room
hablar speak, talk
hace una semana
a week ago
hacer do, make
hacer autostop
hitchhike
hacer cola queue (vb)
hacer dedo hitchhike
hacienda f farmhouse
hamburguesa f
hamburger

harina f flour
hasta even (adv), till, until
¿Hay algo mal/malo?
What is wrong?
hecho/a made
hecho a mano
handmade
helada f frost
helado m ice cream
helicóptero m
helicopter
herida f injury
herido/a injured
hermana f sister
hermano m brother
hernia f hernia
herpes m shingles
herramienta f tool
hervidor m kettle
hervir boil (vb)
hidroala f hydrofoil
hidrodeslizador m
hovercraft
hielo m ice
hierbas fpl herbs
hierro m iron (n, metal)
hígado m liver
hija f daughter
hijo m son
hilado m thread
hilo dental dental floss
hinchado/a swollen
hincharse swell
hinchazón f swelling
hipódromo m race
course
historia f history
histórico/a historic

hoja f leaf
hoja de afeitar razor
  blade
hoja de laurel bay leaf
holandés/holandesa
  m/f Dutch, Dutchman,
  Dutchwoman (adj, n)
hombre m man
hombres men
hombro m shoulder
homosexual gay,
  homosexual
hongo m mushroom
honrado/a honest
hora f hour, time
horario m timetable
horario de apertura
  opening times
horario de visita
  visiting hours
hormiga ant
hornalla f gas cooker
hornillo m cooker
horno m oven
horrible dreadful
hospital m hospital
hospitalidad f
  hospitality
hoy m today
hoyo m hole
hueco m hole
huelga f strike (n)
hueso m bone
huésped/a m/f guest
huevo m egg
huevo de Pascua
  Easter egg

huevos revueltos
  scrambled eggs
humedad f damp (n)
húmedo/a humid
humita bow tie
humo m smoke (n)
humor m humour
húngaro/a m/f
  Hungarian (adj, n)
Hungría Hungary

I

ictericia f jaundice
idea f idea
idioma m language
iglesia f church
igual same (adv)
ilimitado/a unlimited
iluminar light (vb)
imán m magnet
impar odd (number)
imperdible m safety pin
imperfección f flaw
impermeable m
  raincoat
importante great,
  important
imposible impossible
impresos mpl printed
  matter
imprimir print (vb)
impuesto m tax
**Impuesto sobre Valor
  Añadido** Value
  Added Tax
incluido included
incómodo/a
  uncomfortable

inconciente
unconscious
inconveniente f
inconvenience
increíble incredible
indecente nasty
independiente
freelance
indicador de giro
indicator
**indicador de la
gasolina** fuel gauge
indigestión f
indigestion
indio/a m/f Indian
(adj, n)
infección f infection
infeccioso/a infectious
inflamación f
inflammation
inflar pump, inflate
información f
information
informal informal
informar report (vb)
informe m enquiry,
report (n)
ingeniero/a m/f
engineer
Inglaterra England
inglés English
(language)
inglés/inglesa m/f
English, Englishman/
woman (adj, n)
ingredientes mpl
ingredients

inmediatamente
immediately
inscribirse check in
insecto m insect
insistir insist
insolación f sunstroke
insólito/a unusual
insomnio m insomnia
instalación f
connection (telephone)
insulina f insulin
inteligente clever,
intelligent
intentar try
intercambio m
exchange (n)
interesante interesting
intermitente m
indicator
internacional
international
intérprete m/f
interpreter
interruptor m switch
interruptor principal
mains switch
intervalo m interval
introducir introduce,
bring in
inundación f flood
inválido/a disabled
investigación f enquiry,
investigation
invierno m winter
invitación f invitation
invitar invite
inyección f injection
ir go

ir conducir/manejar
  go (by car)
Irlanda Ireland
Irlanda del Norte
  Northern Ireland
irlandés/irlandesa m/f
  Irish, Irishman/woman
  (adj, n)
irse go away
isla f island
Italia Italy
italiano m Italian
  (language)
italiano/a m/f Italian
  (adj, n)
IVA VAT
izquierdo/a left

J

jabalí m boar
jabón m soap
jabón en polvo soap
  powder
jalea f jelly, jam
jamón m ham
jarabe para la tos
  cough mixture
jardín m garden
jardín de infancia
  nursery school
jardín zoológico zoo
jarra f jug
jersey m jersey, jumper,
  pullover
jóven young
joyas fpl jewellery
joyería f jeweller's

jubilado/a m/f old-age
  pensioner, senior citizen
jubilado/a retired
judía f bean
judío/a m/f Jewish, Jew
  (adj, n)
juego m game
juego de fútbol
  football match
jueves m Thursday
juez m/f judge
jugar play (vb, game)
jugo m juice
jugo de fruta fruit juice
jugo de naranja
  orange juice
jugo de tomate
  tomato juice
juguete m toy
julio m July
junio m June
junto a beside
juntos/as together
juntura f joint
jurar swear (an oath)
justo/a fair, just

K

kilo m kilo
kilogramo m kilogram
kilómetro m kilometre

L

la/las the
la mayoría de most
la semana pasada
  a week ago
lado m side

ladrar bark (vb)
ladrillo m brick
ladrón/ladrona m/f
thief, burglar
lago m lake
lámpara f lamp
lamparilla f light bulb
lana f wool
lancha f motorboat
lancha neumática
dinghy
langosta f lobster
lapicera pen, ballpoint
pen
lápiz m pencil
lápiz de labios lipstick
largo/a long (size)
lastimado/a injured
lata f can (n), tin
Latvia Latvia
lavabo m washbasin
lavado de coches
car wash
lavandería f laundry
lavandería automática
launderette, laundromat
lavaplatos m
dishwasher
lavar wash
lavar y marcar
shampoo and set
laxante m laxative
(adj, n)
le it (indirect object)
lección f lesson
leche f milk
leche en polvo
powdered milk

lechuga f lettuce
lechuza f owl
leer read
lejano/a far (adj)
lejos far (adv)
lengua f language,
tongue
lenguado m sole (fish)
lente f lens
lenteja f lentil
lentes m/f glasses,
spectacles, lenses
lentes de contacto
contact lenses
lento/a slow
león m lion
lesbiana f lesbian
(adj, n)
levantar lift (vb)
levantarse get up
ley f law
libra f pound
libre free
libre de impuestos
duty-free
librería f bookshop
libreta de cheques
cheque book
libro m book
libro de frases phrase
book
licencia f licence
licencia de conductor
driving licence
licor m liqueur
licores mpl spirits
(drink)
liebre f hare

ligero/a light (adj, weight)
lima f file (tool), lime
lima de uñas nailfile
límite de velocidad speed limit
limón m lemon
limonada f lemonade
limpiaparabrisas m windscreen wiper
limpiar clean (vb)
limpio/a clean (adj)
lindo/a beautiful
línea f line
lino m linen
linterna f torch
linterna eléctrica flashlight
líquido de freno brake fluid
líquido para lavar washing-up liquid
liquído para remojar soaking solution
lista f list
listo/a clever, ready
litera f couchette
litro m litre
Lituania Lithuania
liviano/a light (adj, weight)
llamada f call (n)
llamada a cobro revertido collect call, reverse-charge call
llamada de larga distancia long-distance call

llamada para despertar wake-up call
llamada telefónica telephone call
llamar call (vb)
llave f key, spanner
llave de contacto/ encendido ignition key
llave de tuercas spanner
llavero m key ring
llaves del coche car keys
llegada f arrival
llegar arrive
llenar fill, fill in, fill up
lleno/a crowded, full, stuffed
llevar lead (vb), wear
llorar cry
lluvia f rain
lo/la it (direct object)
¡Lo siento! Sorry!
lobo m wolf
local local
loco/a mad, crazy
lodo m mud
los dos both
loza f crockery
luces delanteras headlights
lucha f fight (n)
luchar fight (vb)
luego afterwards, later
lugar m place
lujo m luxury

SPANISH → ENGLISH

luna f moon
luna de miel honeymoon
lunes m Monday
lupa f magnifying glass
Luxemburgo Luxembourg
luz f light (n)
luz de freno brake light
luz del sol sunshine

M
madera f wood
madrastra f stepmother
madre f mother
maduro/a ripe
maestro/a m/f teacher
magdalena f bun
malentendido m misunderstanding
maleta f suitcase
maletero m boot, trunk (car)
maletín m briefcase
maletín de primeros auxilios first-aid kit
malo/a awful, mean, bad, nasty, poor (quality)
mancha f stain
mandíbula f jaw
manejar drive
mango m handle
manguera f hose pipe
maní m peanut
mano f hand
manojo m bunch
manta f blanket

mantel m tablecloth
mantequilla f butter
manual m manual (adj, n)
mañana f morning
mañana m tomorrow
mañana por la mañana/tarde/noche tomorrow morning/afternoon/evening
mapa m map
mapa de calles street map
mapa de carreteras road map
máquina f machine
máquina expendedora vending machine
mar m/f sea
Mar Báltico Baltic Sea
Mar del Norte North Sea
maravilloso amazing
marca f brand
marcapasos m pacemaker
marcar dial (vb)
marcha atrás reverse gear
marco m frame
marco de foto picture frame
marea f tide
marea alta high tide
marea baja low tide
mareado/a dizzy, seasick

mareo m travel sickness
marido m husband
mariposa f butterfly
mariscos mpl shellfish
mármol m marble
marrón brown
martillo m hammer
marzo m March
más more
más allá beyond, further
más barato cheaper
más tarde later
máscara f mask
masculino male
mástil m mast
matar kill
matrícula f number plate
mayo m May
mayonesa f mayonnaise
me me
mecánico/a m/f mechanic
mechero m cigarette lighter
media f stocking
mediano/a medium
medianoche f midnight
medias fpl socks, tights
medicamento m drug, medicine
medicina f medicine (science)
médico/a m/f doctor
medida f measure (n)

medieval medieval
medio m middle
medio/a half (adj)
mediodía m midday, noon
medir measure (vb)
mediterráneo/a Mediterranean
medusa f jellyfish
mejilla f cheek
mejillón m mussel
mejor better
mejorar improve
melocotón m peach
melón m melon
mencionar mention
meningitis meningitis
menos less
mensualmente monthly
menta f mint
mente f mind
mentir lie (vb, fib)
mentira f lie (n, untruth)
mentón m chin
menú m menu
menú fijo set menu
mercado m market
merengue m meringue
mermelada f jam, marmalade
mes m month
mesa f table
metal m metal
metro m metre, metro, subway, underground
mezclar mix
mezquita f mosque

SPANISH → ENGLISH

mi my
micro ondas m
  microwave oven
miel f honey
mientras while
miércoles m
  Wednesday
migraña f migraine
mil m thousand
milla f mile
ministro/a m/f minister
minúsculo/a tiny
minusválido/a
  handicapped
minuto m minute (n)
miope short-sighted
mirar look at, watch (vb)
misa f Mass (rel)
mismo/a same (adj)
mitad f half (n)
mitigador painkiller
mochila f backpack
mojado/a wet
molestar annoy, disturb
momento m moment
monasterio m
  monastery
moneda f coin,
  currency
monedero m money
  belt, purse
montaña f mountain
montañismo m
  mountaineering
montar ride
montar en bicicleta
  cycle (vb)
monto m amount

monumento m
  monument
morado m bruise (n)
morado/a purple
morder bite (vb)
morir die
mosquito m mosquito
mostaza f mustard
mostrador m counter
mostrador de
  información
  enquiry desk
mostrar show (vb)
motocicleta f
  motorbike
motor m engine, motor
mover move
mozo/a m/f waiter,
  waitress
muchedumbre f
  crowd
mucho/a long (time), lot,
  much
muchos/muchas
  many
mudarse de casa
  move house
muebles mpl furniture
muelle m quay
muerte f death
muerto/a dead
mugriento/a filthy
mujer f female, lady,
  woman
muletas fpl crutches
multa f fine (n)
mundo m world
muñeca f doll, wrist

SPANISH → ENGLISH

muro m wall
músculo m muscle
museo m museum
músico/a m/f musician
muslo m thigh
**musulmán/
   musulmana** m/f
   Muslim
muy very
muy hecho overdone

N

nacer born
nacimiento m birth
nacional national
nacionalidad f
   nationality
nada nothing
nada más nothing else
nadar swim
nadie nobody
naranja f orange
nariz f nose
nata montada
   whipped cream
natillas fpl custard
natural natural
naturaleza f nature
náusea f nausea
navaja de afeitar
   razor
navegación f sailing
navegar sail
Navidad f Christmas
neblina f fog, mist
necesario/a necessary
necesidad f need (n)
necesitar need (vb)

negativo m negative
   (n, photo)
negocios mpl business
negro/a black
neocelandés New
   Zealander
neumático m tyre
**neumático de
   repuesto** spare tyre
neumático sin aire
   flat tyre
nevera f fridge
nevera portátil cool
   bag, cool box
ni ... ni neither ... nor
nido m nest
niebla f fog
nieta f granddaughter
nieto m grandson
nieve, está nevando
   snow, it is snowing
ninguno/a none
niña f girl
niñera f nanny
niño m boy
niño/a m/f child
no no, not
no contiene azúcar
   sugar-free
no fumador/a non-
   smoking
no funciona out of
   order
no importa it doesn't
   matter
no puedo couldn't
noche f late evening,
   night

Nochebuena f
  Christmas Eve
Nochevieja f New
  Year's Eve
nombre m name
nombre de pila
  Christian name, first
  name
nombre de soltera
  maiden name
norte m north
Noruega Norway
noruego/a m/f
  Norwegian (adj, n)
nos us
nosotros/as us, we
nota f note
noticias fpl news
novela f novel
novia f bride, fiancée,
  girlfriend
noviembre m
  November
novio m bridegroom,
  fiancé, boyfriend
nube f cloud
nuera f daughter-in-law
nuestro/a our
Nueva Zelanda New
  Zealand
nuevo/a new
nuez f nut, walnut
número m number, size
número de clave
  pin number
**número de
  inscripción**
  registration number

número de teléfono
  phone number
nunca never

O

o or
o ... o either ... or
obligatorio/a
  compulsory
obra f play (n, theatre)
obtener get, obtain
océano m ocean
octubre m October
oculista m/f
  ophthalmologist
ocupación f occupation
ocupado/a busy,
  engaged, occupied
oeste m west
oficina f office
oficina de cambio
  bureau de change
oficina de correos
  post office
oído m ear
oír hear
ojalá hopefully
ojo m eye
ojotas fpl sandals
ola f wave
oler smell
olvidar forget
ópera f opera
operación f operation
operador/a m/f
  operator (phone)
operador de turismo
  tour operator

oporto m port (wine)
óptico/a m/f optician
opuesto/a opposite
orden m order (n)
ordenador m
   computer
orilla f hem, shore
oro m gold
orquesta f orchestra
oscuro/a dark
otoño m autumn
otra vez again
otro/a other, another
oveja f sheep
oxidado/a rusty

P

paciente m/f patient
   (adj, n)
padrastro m stepfather
padre m father
padres mpl parents
pagadero/a due
pagado/a paid
pagar pay
página f page
páginas amarillas
   yellow pages
pago m payment
país m country
paisaje m scenery
Países Bajos
   Netherlands
paja f straw
pajarita f bow tie
pájaro m bird
pala f spade
palabra f word

palabrota f swear-word
palacio m palace
palanca f handle, lever
palanca de cambios
   gear lever
pálido/a pale
palo de golf golf club
   (stick)
pan m bread
pan de centeno rye
   bread
pan integral de trigo
   wholemeal bread
panadería f bakery
pantalla f screen
pantalones mpl pants,
   trousers
pantalones cortos
   mpl shorts
pantano m marsh
panty m pantyhose
pañal m diaper, nappy
pañales descartables
   disposable diapers/
   nappies
paño m cloth, duster
paño para el suelo
   floorcloth
pañuelo m
   handkerchief
papa f potato
papas fritas fpl chips,
   crisps, French fries
papel m paper
papel de carta
   notepaper
papel de envolver
   wrapping paper

papel de escribir writing paper

papel metálico tinfoil

papelería f stationer's

paperas fpl mumps

paquete m package, packet, parcel

par m pair

para for (purpose)

parabrisas m windscreen

parachoques m fender

parada f stopover

parada de autobús bus stop

parada de taxis taxi rank

parador m hostel

paraguas m umbrella

parar stay, stop

pardo/a brown

pare stop sign

parecido/a similar

pared f wall

pareja f couple

parejo/a even (adj)

pariente m/f relative, relation

parque m park (n)

parquímetro m parking meter

parte f part, portion

parte de arriba top

parte de repuesto spare part

partes del coche car parts

partido m match (sport), party (political)

partido de fútbol football match

pasa f raisin

pasado m past

pasado/a de moda old-fashioned

pasajero/a m/f passenger

pasaporte m passport

pasar happen, pass, spend (time)

paseo a caballo horse riding

pasillo m aisle, corridor

paso de peatones pedestrian crossing

pastel m cake, pastry, pie

pastelería f cake shop

pastilla f pill

pastilla para dormir sleeping pill

pastillas para la garganta throat lozenges

patata f potato

patatas fritas fpl chips, crisps, French fries

patear kick

patín m skate (n)

patinar skate (vb)

patines mpl ice skates

patio de recreo playground

pato/a m/f duck

SPANISH → ENGLISH

patrón m pattern
pavo m turkey
peaje m toll
peatón m pedestrian
pecho m breast, chest
peculiar peculiar
pedal m pedal
pedazo m piece
pedido m request (n)
pedir order, request (vb)
pegado stuck
pegamento m glue
pegar stick (vb)
peinar comb (vb)
peine m comb (n)
pelar peel (vb)
pelea f fight (n)
pelear fight, quarrel (vb)
película f film (n)
peligro m danger
peligroso/a dangerous
pelo m hair
peluca f wig
peluquería f
  hairdresser's
peluquero/a m/f
  hairdresser
pena f pity
pendientes mpl
  earrings
península f peninsula
pensar think
pensión f bed &
  breakfast, boarding
  house, guesthouse
pensión completa full
  board
peor worse

pepino m cucumber
pequeño/a little, small
pera f pear
percha f hanger
percha para abrigo
  coat hanger
perder lose
perdido/a lost, missing
¡Perdón! Excuse me!
perezoso/a lazy
perfecto/a perfect
perfume m perfume
periódico m
  newspaper
período m period
perla f pearl
permanente f perm
permiso m licence,
  permit (n)
permiso de caza
  hunting permit
permiso de pesca
  fishing permit
permitir let, allow,
  permit (vb)
pero but
perro/a m/f dog
persiana blind (n)
persona f person
pesado/a dull, boring,
  heavy
pesar weigh
pescadería f
  fishmonger's
pescado m fish
peso m weight
petición f request (n)
piano m piano

picadura f sting (n)
picadura de insecto insect bite
picar itch, sting (vb)
picnic m picnic
pico m peak
picor m itch (n)
pie m foot
piedra f stone
piel f fur, leather, peel, skin
pierna f leg
pies mpl feet
pieza f piece
pijamas m pyjamas
piloto m pilot
pimienta f pepper (spice)
pimiento m pepper (vegetable)
pinchazo m puncture
pintar paint (vb)
pintura f paint (n)
pintura de uñas nail varnish/polish
pinza f clothes peg
pinzas fpl tweezers
piña f pineapple
pipa f pipe (smoking)
pirulí lollipop
piscina f pool
piscina climatizada/cubierta indoor pool
piso m apartment, flat, floor, storey
pista de hielo ice rink
pista de patinaje skating rink

pista de tenis tennis court
pista para esquiar ski slope
pistas para principiantes nursery slope
plancha f iron (n, appliance)
planchar iron (vb)
planta f plant, storey
planta baja ground floor
plástico/a plastic
plástico para envolver cling film
plata f silver
plataforma f platform
platillo m saucer
platinos mpl points (car)
plato m dish, plate
plato principal main course
playa f beach
playa nudista nudist beach
plaza f square
plomero/a m plumber
plomo m lead (n, metal)
población f population
pobre poor (impecunious)
pocillo m cup
poco a poco gradually
poco hecho underdone

poco profundo/a
shallow

pocos/pocas m/f few,
a few

poder can (vb), may,
might

¿Podría? Could I?

podrido/a rotten

polaco/a m/f Polish,
Pole (adj, n)

policía f police

polilla f moth

pollo m chicken

Polonia Poland

polvo m dust, powder

polvo de lavar
washing powder

pomada f ointment

poner put

popular popular

por by, for, because of,
per, through, via

por adelantado in
advance

por aquí this way

por ejemplo for
example

por favor please

por horas hourly (adv)

por la mañana a.m.
(before noon)

por la noche overnight

por la tarde p.m.
(after noon)

¿Por qué? Why?

por su cuenta
freelance

por suerte fortunately

por supuesto
absolutely, definitely

por todas partes
everywhere

porcelana f china

porción f portion

porque because

portaequipaje m
luggage rack, roof-rack

portero m doorman

portero/a m/f
caretaker, porter

Portugal Portugal

**portugués/
portuguesa** m/f
Portuguese (adj, n)

posada f inn

posible possible

postal f postcard

poste indicador
signpost

póster m poster

postre m dessert,
pudding

práctica f practice

practicar practise

precio m price

precio barato cheap
rate

**precio de temporada
alta** peak rate

precioso/a beautiful,
lovely

preferir prefer

prefijo m dialling code

pregunta f question

preguntar ask

premio m prize

SPANISH → ENGLISH

preocupado/a worried
presentar introduce (people)
presente present (adj)
preservativo m condom
presión f pressure
presión alta (sangre) high blood pressure
presión arterial blood pressure
presión en los neumáticos tyre pressure
prestar lend
primavera f spring (season)
primer nombre first name
primer piso m first floor
primer/a ministro/a m/f prime minister
primera clase first class
primero/a first
primeros auxilios first aid
primo/a m/f cousin
principal main
principiante m/f beginner
prismáticos mpl binoculars
privado/a private
probablemente probably
probarse try on
problema m problem

problemas mpl trouble
profesor/a m/f teacher
profundo/a deep
programa m programme, program
prohibido/a forbidden, prohibited
promedio average
promesa f promise (n)
prometer promise (vb)
prometido/a m/f fiancé, fiancée
pronóstico del tiempo weather forecast
pronto soon
pronunciar pronounce
propiedad perdida lost property
propietario/a m/f landlord/landlady, owner
propina f service charge, tip, gratuity
protestante m/f Protestant
próximo/a next
público/a public
pueblo m village
¿Puedo? Could I?
puente m bridge
puerco m/f pig
puerro m leek
puerta f door, gate
puerto m port, harbour
puesto m stall
pulga f flea
pulgada f inch
pulgar m thumb

pulir polish (vb)
pulmón m lung
pulsera f bracelet
puntada f stitch
puntilla f lace
punto m point (n)
pura vida OK, very well
puré de papas/patatas mashed potatoes
puro m cigar

Q

¿Qué? Pardon? What?
que hace juego matching
¿Qué hora es? What's the time?
¿Qué pasa? What's the matter?
¡Qué pena! It's a pity
¿Qué tal? How do you do? How are you?
quedarse remain, stay
queja f complaint
quejarse complain
quemadura de sol sunburn
quemar burn
querer want
querido/a dear
queso m cheese
¿Quién? Who?
quieto still (quiet)
quincena f fortnight
quiosko m kiosk, news stand
quiste m cyst

quitaesmalte nail polish remover
quizás maybe, perhaps

R

rábano m radish
rabia f rabies
radiador m radiator
radio f radio
radiografía f X-ray
rallado/a grated
rana f frog
rancio/a stale
rápidamente quickly
rápido/a fast
raqueta f racket
raqueta de tenis tennis racket
raro/a foreign, strange, odd, rare, weird
rascar scratch (vb)
rasgado torn
rastrillo m rake
rata f rat
ratero/a m/f pickpocket
ratón m mouse
rayado/a striped
rayo m lightning, spoke (of wheel)
raza f race (people)
razonable reasonable
real real, royal
realmente really
rebajas fpl sale
rebanada f slice
rebeca f cardigan
recado m message

SPANISH → ENGLISH

SPANISH → ENGLISH

recalentar overheat
recargar recharge
recaudador/a m/f
  receiver (tax)
recepción f reception
recepcionista m/f
  receptionist
receta f prescription,
  recipe
rechazar refuse (vb)
recibo m receipt
recientemente
  recently
recogedor m dustpan
recoger collect
**recolección de
  equipajes** baggage
  reclaim
recomendar
  recommend
reconocer recognize
recordar remember
recuerdo m souvenir
red f net, web
redondo/a round
reducción f reduction
reducir reduce
reembolsar refund (vb)
reembolso m
  refund (n)
reemplazo de cadera
  hip replacement
refractario/a
  ovenproof
refresco m soft drink
refrigerador m fridge
regalar present (vb)

regalo m gift,
  present (n)
regalo de boda
  wedding present
**regalo de
  cumpleaños**
  birthday present
región f region
registrar check, inspect
registrarse check in
registro m register (n)
regla f ruler
regresar come back,
  return
reina f queen
Reino Unido United
  Kingdom
reír laugh (vb)
relámpago flash (of
  lightning)
relleno/a stuffed
relleno m filling
  (sandwich)
reloj m clock, watch
remar row (vb)
remendar mend
remo m oar
remolcar tow
remolque m caravan,
  trailer
reparación f repair (n)
reparar fix, repair (vb)
repelente de insectos
  insect repellent
repetir repeat
repleto/a crowded
repollo m cabbage

representación f
performance
**representante de
ventas** sales
representative
República Checa
Czech Republic
**República de
Eslovaquia** Slovak
Republic
requerir require
resaca f hangover
resbaladizo/a slippery
resbalarse slip
rescate m rescue (n)
rescate de montaña
mountain rescue
reserva f reservation
reserva natural nature
reserve
reservar reserve
residente m/f resident
(adj, n)
residuo m waste
resistente al horno
ovenproof
respetuoso/a polite
respirar breathe
responder answer (vb)
respuesta f answer,
reply (n)
resto m rest
(remainder)
retirado/a retired
retrato m portrait
reuma m rheumatism
reunión f meeting
revelación f exposure

revelado film
processing
revés m reverse (n)
revisor/a m/f ticket
collector
revista f magazine
rey m king
rezar pray
rico/a delicious, rich
ridículo/a ridiculous
rímel m mascara
riña f quarrel (n)
riñón m kidney
río m river
risa f laugh (n)
rizado/a curly
robado mugged, stolen
robar steal
roble m oak
robo m break-in,
burglary, theft
roca f rock
rodeado surrounded
rodilla f knee
rojo/a red
rollo m coil (n, rope)
romper break
ron m rum
roncar snore
ropa f clothing, gear
ropa de cama bed
linen
ropa de hombre
menswear
ropa de mujer ladies'
wear
ropa interior lingerie,
underpants, underwear

SPANISH → ENGLISH

SPANISH → ENGLISH

ropas fpl clothes
ropero m cupboard
rosa f rose (flower)
rosa m pink
rosquilla f doughnut
roto/a broken
rotonda f roundabout
rubeola f German measles, rubella
rubio/a fair (hair colour)
rueda f wheel
ruido m noise
ruidoso/a loud, noisy
ruina f ruin

S

sábado m Saturday
sábana f sheet
saber know
sabor m flavour
sacacorcho m corkscrew
saco de dormir sleeping bag
sagrado/a holy
sal f salt
sala f hall, ward (hospital)
sala de embarque departure lounge
sala de espera waiting room
sala de estar living room, lounge
sala municipal town hall
salado/a savoury
salario m wage

salchicha f sausage
salida f departure, exit
salida de emergencia emergency exit, fire exit
salir depart, leave
salmón m salmon
salmón ahumado smoked salmon
salón m lounge
salón de belleza beauty salon
salsa f gravy, sauce
saltar jump (vb)
salto m jump (n)
salto de esquí ski jump
¡Salud! Cheers!
saludable healthy
saludo m greeting
salvar rescue (vb)
sandalia f sandal
sandía f watermelon
sandwich m sandwich
sangrar bleed
sangre f blood
sapo m toad
sarampión m measles
sartén f frying pan
sastre m tailor
se puede romper breakable
secador de pelo hairdryer
secadora f dryer, spin-dryer
secar blow-dry
sección f department
seco/a dry

secretario/a m/f
  secretary
seda f silk
seguir follow
segunda clase
  second-class
segunda mano
  second-hand
segundo/a second
seguro m insurance
**seguro contra
  terceros** third-party
  insurance
seguro de coche car
  insurance
seguro de vida life
  insurance
seguro médico
  medical insurance
seguro/a safe (adj),
  sure
sello m stamp, postage
  stamp
semáforo m traffic light
semana f week
semana pasada last
  week
semana próxima next
  week
Semana Santa Easter
semanalmente weekly
sencillo/a simple
sendero m path,
  footpath
sendero de bicicletas
  cycle track
sentarse sit

sentencia f sentence
  (law)
sentir feel
señal f signal
señal de marcar
  dialling tone
señal de tráfico road
  sign
señalar point (vb)
señor m Mr
señora f Mrs, lady
señorita f Miss, Ms
separado/a separate
séptico/a septic
septiembre m
  September
ser be
serio/a serious
serpiente f snake
servicio m service
servicio de caballeros
  gents' toilet
**servicio de courier/
  entrega** courier
  service
servicio de damas
  ladies' toilet
servicios mpl bath-
  room, cloakroom,
  lavatory, toilet
servilleta f napkin,
  serviette
servilletas de papel
  paper napkins/serviettes
servir pour
sexo m sex
si if
sí yes

SPANISH → ENGLISH

si no otherwise, if not
sidra f cider
siempre always
siga derecho straight on
siglo m century
significar mean, intend
silencio m silence
silla f chair
silla alta high chair
silla de montar saddle
silla de patio deck chair
silla de ruedas pushchair, wheelchair
sillón m armchair
simpático/a friendly
simple plain
simular fake (vb)
sin without
sin alcohol non-alcoholic
sin camiseta topless
sin plomo lead-free
sinagoga f synagogue
sobre above, on, over
sobre m envelope
sobrina f niece
sobrino m nephew
sobrio/a sober
socio/a m/f partner (business)
socorrista m/f lifeguard
soda f soda
sofá m couch
soga f rope
sol m sun

solamente just, only
soleado/a sunny
solicitud f request (n)
solo alone, single
sólo only (adv)
soltero/a single
soluble soluble
sombra f shade
sombra de ojos eye shadow
sombrero m hat
sombrilla f sunshade
somnífero m sleeping pill
son are
sonar ring (vb)
sonreír smile (vb)
sopa f soup
sordo/a deaf
sostén m bra
sótano m basement
su her, his
suave soft
subir climb, get on
submarinismo m scuba diving
subterráneo m tunnel
subterráneo/a underground (adj)
subtítulo m subtitle
sucio/a dirty, nasty
sucursal f branch (office)
Sudáfrica South Africa
sudafricano/a South African (adj, n)
sudar sweat (vb)
Suecia f Sweden

sueco/a m/f Swedish,
Swede (adj, n)
suegra f mother-in-law
suegro m father-in-law
suegros mpl in-laws,
parents-in-law
suela f sole (shoe)
sueldo m wage
suelo m floor (of room)
suelto/a loose
suerte f luck
suéter m jumper,
sweater
suficiente plenty,
enough
Suiza Switzerland
suizo/a m/f Swiss
(adj, n)
suizo-alemán Swiss-
German
superior up-market
suplemento m
supplement
sur m south
suspensión f
suspension

T
tabla de planchar
ironing board
tabla de surfear
surfboard
tablilla f shingle
tablón de anuncios
noticeboard
tal vez maybe, perhaps
taladro m drill (n)
talco m talcum powder

talla media medium
sized
talón m heel
tamaño m size
también also, too
tampón m tampon
tanque m tank
tanque séptico septic
tank
tapa f lid
tapado jammed
tapón m plug (bath)
tarde late
tarde f afternoon, early
evening
tarea f housework
tarifa f fare
tarjeta f card
tarjeta de crédito
charge card, credit card
tarjeta de cumpleaños
birthday card
tarjeta de embarque
boarding card
tarjeta de identidad
identity card
**tarjeta de identidad
bancario** cheque
card
tarjeta de llamadas
phone card
tarta f cake
taxi m cab, taxi
taxista m/f taxi driver
taza f cup
tazón m mug
té m tea

té de hierbas, té natural herbal tea
teatro m theatre
techo m roof
techo corredizo sunroof
tejer knit
tejido m knitwear, material, fabric
teleférico m cable car
teléfono m phone, telephone
teléfono móvil mobile phone
teléfono pago/público payphone
televisión f television
temperatura f temperature
templo m temple
temporada f season
temporario temporary
tendedero m clothes line
tendón m tendon
tenedor m fork
tener have, hold
tener miedo be afraid of
tener que have to
tener sed thirsty
tener suerte lucky
tengo dolor it's sore
tenis m tennis
tentempié m snack
teñir dye (vb)
termas fpl hot spring
terminal m terminal

terminar finish (vb)
termo m flask
termómetro m thermometer
ternera f calf, veal
terremoto m earthquake
terrible awful
terrón m lump
testigo m/f witness
teta f breast
tetera f teapot
tetina f teat (bottle)
tía f aunt
tiempo m weather
tienda f shop, store, food shop
tienda de alimentos naturales health food shop
tienda de departamentos department store
tierra f earth, ground, land
tijeras fpl scissors
tijeras para uñas nail scissors
timbre m doorbell
tímido/a shy
timón m rudder
tinta f ink
tinte m dye (n)
tintorería f dry cleaner's
tío m uncle
típico/a typical
tipo m sort, type

tipo de cambio rate of exchange
tirante tight
tirar pull
tisú m tissue
título degree (qualification)
toalla f towel
tobillo m ankle
toca discos CD player
tocino m bacon
todavía still (yet)
todo everything
todo m whole (n)
todo junto altogether
todos/todas m/f everyone
tomar take
tomar prestado borrow
tomate m tomato
tonto/a silly
torcedura f sprain (n)
torcer sprain (vb)
tormenta f storm, thunderstorm
tornillo m nut (for bolt), screw
torre f tower
tortilla f omelette
tos f cough (n)
toser cough (vb)
total m total
totalmente completely
trabajar work
trabajar por cuenta propia self-employed
trabajo m job

trabajo doméstico housework
traducción f translation
traducir translate
traductor/a m/f translator
traer bring, fetch
tráfico m traffic
tragar swallow (vb)
traje m suit
traje de agua wetsuit
traje de baño/ bañador swimming costume
trampolín m diving board
tranquilo/a quiet
transbordador m ferry
transbordador de coches car ferry
transpiración f sweat (n)
tranvía m tram
trapo m duster, rag, floorcloth
trapo de cocina dishtowel
trato m deal
travesía f journey
tren m train
trenza f plait
trineo m sledge
triste sad
trotar jog (vb)
trote m jog (n)
trozo m lump
trucha f trout
trueno m thunder

SPANISH → ENGLISH

tú you
tu your
tubo m tube
tubo de escape
  exhaust pipe
tubo de respiración
  snorkel
tubo interno inner tube
tumbona f deck chair
túnel m tunnel
turco/a m/f Turkish,
  Turk (adj, n)
turismo m
  sightseeing
turquesa f turquoise
Turquía Turkey

U

úlcera f ulcer
úlcera de boca mouth
  ulcer
último/a last
un poco bit
una vez once
uniforme even (adj)
Unión Europea EU
unirse join
universidad f
  university
uno m one
unos/unas some
uña f nail
urgencias casualty
  department
urgente urgent
usar use, wear
utensilios de cocina
  cooking utensils

útil useful
uvas fpl grapes

V

vaca f cow
vacaciones fpl
  vacation, holidays
vacaciones
  organizadas
  package holiday
vacío/a empty
vacuna f vaccine
vago/a lazy
vagón m carriage
vainilla f vanilla
¡Vale! OK!
vale all right
vale m voucher
válido/a valid
valle m valley
valor m value
válvula f valve
vapor m steam
varicela f chicken pox
varios/as several
vaso m glass (tumbler)
vasto/a great
vecino/a m/f neighbour
vegetales mpl
  vegetables
vegetariano/a m/f
  vegetarian
vehículo m vehicle
vela f candle
velocidad f speed
velocímetro m
  speedometer
vena f vein

vencer expire
venda f bandage
vendaje m dressing, bandage
vendedor/a m/f salesperson
vender sell
veneno m poison
venenoso/a poisonous
venir come
ventana f window
ventilador m fan
ventoso/a windy
ver see
verano m summer
verdadero/a true
verde green
verdulería greengrocer's
verduras fpl vegetables
verduras orgánicas organic vegetables
vereda f sidewalk
vergüenza f shame
vestíbulo m lobby
vestido m dress
vestido de noche nightdress
vestuario m changing room
veterinario/a m/f vet, veterinarian
vía via
viajar travel
viaje m journey, tour
viaje de negocios business trip

viaje en barco boat trip
vida f life
vidriera f shop window
viejo/a ancient, old
Viena Vienna
viento m wind
viernes m Friday
Viernes Santo Good Friday
vinagre m vinegar
vinagreta f salad dressing
vino m wine
vino de la casa house wine
vino de mesa table wine
vino medio seco medium dry wine
vino tinto red wine
viñedo m vineyard
violación f rape (n)
violar rape (vb)
violeta f violet (adj, n)
virus m virus
visa f visa
visita guiada guided tour
visitante m/f visitor
visitar visit
vista f sight, view
vitrina f shop window
viudo/a m/f widower, widow
vivero m nursery (plants)
vivir live

SPANISH → ENGLISH

vivo/a lively
volante m steering wheel
volar fly (vb)
volcán m volcano
voltaje m voltage
volver go back, return, turn, come back
vomitar vomit
¡Voy a vomitar! I'm going to be sick!
voz f voice
vuelo m flight
vuelo chárter charter flight
vuelo de conexión connecting flight
vuelo libre hang-gliding

Y
y and
ya already
yate m yacht
yema f yolk
yerno m son-in-law
yeso m plaster
yo I
yo estoy I am
yo mismo myself
yo soy I am

Z
zanahoria f carrot
zapatillas fpl slippers
zapato m shoe
zona f zone
zorro/a m/f fox
zumo m juice
zumo de fruta fruit juice
zumo de naranja orange juice
zurdo/a left-handed

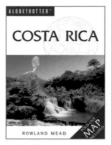

GLOB

Costa Rican
Spanish
In Your Pocket

Phrase Book
Useful phrases for specific situations,
from booking a hotel room
to finding a hospital

◆

Dictionary
A handy two-way dictionary that
will help you understand as
well as being understood

◆

Includes basic grammar,
pronunciation, etiquette and general
information about Costa Rica

Published and distributed by
New Holland Publishers (UK) Ltd London

£3.99

ISBN 1-84537-292-1

$6.95
Globe Pequot

BK01522699